Pauline Collett.

11 . 10 . 86 .

'... he has the air of the great navigator, afloat in a gallant ship on adventurous voyages of the spirit.'

Introduction to the Music of Elgar
— W R Anderson

An Elgar Travelogue

written and illustrated by
Pauline Collett

Thames Publishing
14 Barlby Road, London, W10 6AR

ISBN 0 905210 21 2

Printed by Knight and Forster, Leeds

Contents

Acknowledgements

I am greatly indebted to the following people, who have kindly supplied me with helpful information for this book:

Mr E Wulstan Atkins, Mr Dennis Clark, Mr Michael Derbyshire, Mrs H Joyce Hicks, Mrs Gladys M Lawson, Mr William R Mitchell, Mr Raymond Monk, Dr Jerrold Northrop Moore, Mr W Morris, Mr and Mrs Peter Parsons, Rev E Hugh Seal, Mrs Marion Simmons, Rev Tom Taylor and Mr Alan Webb. I owe a special debt to Mr Geoffrey Hodgkins, who has generously allowed me to include information from his own researches on Elgar's visit to Llangranog. My thanks are also due to the following people, who have given or loaned me photographs: Mr Ian Lace, Dr William L Reed, Mrs Marion Simmons, Mrs Jenny Stacey, Mr Michael Trott and Mr and Mrs David Watt. I am most grateful to Mr H V Cartwright for allowing me to reproduce the photograph of the Via Edward Elgar, Alassio; to the North Craven Heritage Trust for permission to use the photograph of Settle Market Place; and to Mr Raymond Monk for the photographs reproduced as the frontispiece and on page 93, from his private collection. The remaining old photographs and postcards are reproduced by kind permission of the Elgar Birthplace Trust. My sincere thanks go to Mr Jack McKenzie, formerly Curator of the Elgar Birthplace Museum, for all his help; to Mrs Margaret Preston for typing the manuscript; and to my husband, Barry, for the photographs appearing on pages 48 and 65 and for his valuable advice and assistance in bringing this book to fruition.

Pauline Collett

Illustrations

*   *   *

Music examples reproduced by permission of Novello and Company.

Introduction

Elgar, more than most great composers, was affected by his environment to the extent that it had a profound influence on his state of mind and resulting compositions. Many of his works were the direct result of visits to different places or areas, and this book traces the periods of time he spent with friends, his holidays in this country and his trips abroad.

From his earliest days Elgar had been a traveller, accompanying his father in his pony and trap to outlying country houses on his rounds as a piano tuner. Later in life he was to travel much further afield: to local spots on his bicycle; around the country by steam train and motor car; by packet steamer and ocean liner to foreign parts — and even, once, by aeroplane — such was the speed of the development of transport in his lifetime.

The following pages have been divided into three parts. The first section, 'Friends Visited', includes the people with whom he sought companionship or with whom he stayed during festivals — and most were long-lived friendships — and whose homes provided refuge and relaxation. Also included in this section is his sister Polly, whose home was always a sanctuary when life became unbearable. To many of these friends he was to dedicate his music. Had it not been for 'Hasfield Court', his 'friends pictured within' the *Enigma Variations* would have taken on a different aspect, for it was through his visits here that he was to meet William Meath Baker, Richard Baxter Townshend and Dorabella.

The second section deals with the holidays Elgar spent, both as a bachelor and after his marriage, in Great Britain, usually for relatively short periods of time and often for health reasons.

Part three deals with the holidays and conducting engagements abroad, these vacations often spanning several weeks or even months. Despite continual financial worries and the fact that their daughter Carice had often to be left behind, especially during her schooldays, the Elgars were fortunate enough to be able to spend a good deal of time abroad, often trying to avoid the British winter, which Elgar hated, but not always being successful in escaping bad weather. They made slow, lengthy journeys, often felt ill, but nevertheless appeared to have unlimited energy for concert-going, visiting ancient monuments and museums, and being entertained.

Of necessity they were partly working holidays for Elgar, much of his time often being spent orchestrating or correcting proofs. From many of these holiday experiences, however, new music resulted, music giving insight into the places visited — the Bavarian songs, the overture *In the South* (Alassio) or the piano piece *In Smyrna*, music not based on folk melodies cribbed from foreign parts but Elgarian through and through.

PART I
FRIENDS VISITED

'The Elms', Stoke Prior, near Bromsgrove, Worcestershire

Susannah Mary Elgar, or Polly as she was always known, was born in 1855, two years before Edward. By 1877 she had made her debut as a soprano soloist and the following year she was in the chorus of the Three Choirs Festival, Edward and his father being part of the second violin section of the orchestra. In 1879, Polly married William Grafton and moved into a house at 35, Chestnut Walk, Worcester, called 'Loretto Villa'. Shortly afterwards Edward moved in as a lodger and stayed with the couple for the next five years. They were a sensible and industrious pair and in 1883 William was given the opportunity of an official residence at Stoke Prior, near Bromsgrove, where he was manager of the salt works. When they moved, Edward went to live with his sister Lucy and her husband, Charles Pipe.

'The Elms' was the name of the Grafton's new residence. It was a spacious black-and-white farmhouse above the Stoke works, with some farmland attached. Polly had five children: Gerald, Roland, May, Madeline (Madge) and Clare. Elgar often visited the family here and became very fond of his nephews and nieces. In later years Madge and May particularly were to be a great help and comfort to him. In this congenial atmosphere Elgar found it easy to relax, but he would often help Polly with a works concert or play the violin for some local charity. Throughout his life he continued to return to 'The Elms' for rest and relaxation.

On June 22 1904, Elgar received news that he was to be made a Knight. At that time his ageing father was staying with Polly at Stoke

Prior. The following day Elgar went straight to 'The Elms' to tell his father and the family the news. The life here always seemed a tonic to him and he loved its surroundings. In 1913, after feeling unwell for some time, he was sent by his doctor to see a consultant at St Bartholomew's Hospital who pronounced him physically fit and recommended more golf! Elgar immediately left for Stoke in the hope of recuperation.

When the Elgars moved to 'Severn House' in London, Elgar, often longing for his native countryside, would return to stay with the Graftons for a few days at a time, four or five times a year. During April 1916 he was suffering a great deal from the strain of overwork. He set off to Stoke for his usual few days' rest, but he had to be taken from the train at Oxford by a certain Captain Dillon, as he was feeling giddy. He was put into the Acland Nursing Home, where he had to stay for three days suffering from an attack of Ménièr's Disease.

In 1917 his great friend Alice Stuart-Wortley (whom Elgar often called 'Windflower') had been visiting some of Elgar's old haunts, including Stoke Prior. Referring to this visit he wrote to her:

> I am glad you 'feel' Stoke. That is a place where I see & *hear* (yes!) you. A. [ie, his wife] has not been there since *1888* & does not care to go & no one of my friends has ever been but you. No one has seen my fields & my 'common' & my trees, only the Windflower, and I found her namesakes growing there — aborigines I'm sure — real pure sweet forest folk. Bless you.[1]

It was natural, therefore, that it was to Stoke that Elgar should flee after the death of his wife in 1920, although it seems strange that Alice had no desire to visit her sister-in-law's home after her marriage. Here Elgar found he could escape a little from his memories:

> I am doing my best here — the weather of course prevents me having any walks but Juno seems to know that something is wrong & never leaves me — such wonderful things are dogs. Here my dear A. never came so I can bear the sight of the roads & fields ...[2]

At the same time he was to discover that Polly, a widow since 1907, was being turned out of her home. He continues:

> After 37 years my poor old sister may have to turn out — everything being sold — & although the 70 acres or so of land has been let with an ʳ· farm for more than 200 years the new rich refuse to sell the house

---

[1] *Portrait of Elgar*, Michael Kennedy, p 273
[2] Letter to Frank Schuster, April 17 1920

& paddock separately — after 200 years! All the consideration she was treated with as the widow of a respected (& beloved) manager is thrown to the winds — so I am in a sad house.

Three months later, after the advertisement for the sale of 'The Elms' had appeared, Elgar wrote to Alice Stuart-Wortley on July 18:

The old life is over and everything seems blotted out ...

It seems odd that Stoke was advertised last Saturday week — the *same* day as Birchwood Lodge (our old Worcester cottage) advertised & *sold* — I wanted it, & then in Country Life same day!! all the Wye fishing where you & I walked once. Does it not seem strange that the *three* only havens of rest, to which in my busy life I have always fled for comfort & rest, should all be sold in the same week?

Later he wrote to her again:

About Stoke — I asked a millionaire friend — I descended so low — & I begged he wd. save it: he sympathised & sent an agent who reported it wd. only pay *four per cent* — so my friend could not entertain it!!! That is the end: the public have all my best work for nothing & I have not one single friend who cares — except you! My whole past is wiped out & I am quite alone.[1]

As early as 1892 Elgar had written a work for May Grafton called *Very Melodious Exercises in The First Position*. In 1924 he wrote a *March* for violin, 'cello and piano for the Grafton family and in 1932 dedicated a *Sonatina* for pianoforte to May.

'The Elms', Stoke Prior.

---

[1] *Portrait of Elgar*, op cit, p 290

Giggleswick and Settle, North Yorkshire

Elgar first met Dr Charles William Buck of Settle at a British Medical Association Conference held in the Shirehall in Worcester in 1882. It was music that brought the two men into a life-long friendship which extended over some fifty years. Elgar's *Air de Ballet* was played by the orchestra, of which Buck was a member, at the Jubilee concert. They were introduced by John Beare, a mutual friend, who was the son of a Settle lawyer and a music dealer in London. As an instrument maker he had done business with the Elgar Brothers and became a family friend.[1] The rapport between Elgar and Buck was immediate, and later that summer Buck invited Elgar to spend a holiday in Giggleswick. It was to become the first of many regular visits.

Charles Buck was born in 1851 and educated at Giggleswick School and Owen's College, Manchester. He set up in practice in 1876. His surgery was in a large three-storey house standing in Settle Market Place, now the premises of the National Westminster Bank. Here he gave consultations, mixed medicines and occasionally pulled out teeth using gas. His outlying patients were visited on horseback, or he was driven by his coachman in his pony and trap, with its folding hood which could be raised in bad weather — for the winds on Malham Moor, over 1,000 feet above sea level, could be biting cold. In the evening after supper he would have a glass of beer and then smoke his pipe, filling four or five at a time before a session of music-making, so that he would not have to be distracted by refilling a single pipe.

Buck was a devoted amateur musician, playing both the viola and the 'cello in orchestras and chamber groups, and he was a keen collector of local folk-songs. He also conducted the Settle Orchestra.

During these visits, Elgar and Buck played a good deal of chamber music together and often Elgar would discuss his compositions with his friend. The two men played golf and tennis and explored much of the surrounding limestone country of North Craven, such as Giggleswick Scar and Malham Cove, the Dales, the Pennines and the Lake District. They corresponded continually in the early days of their friendship and Buck sent Elgar photographs of Catterick Force and

---

[1] He was also one of Elgar's early publishers

Scaleber Force after their visits there, which Elgar subsequently put up in his room. On receiving the Catterick photograph Elgar wrote:

> Catterick Force is duly installed in a place of honour next to Scaleber (received last year), and the violence done to Settle geography is more than recompensed by the pretty contrast presented ...[1]

As an old man, Elgar was to remember these holidays with great pleasure. On August 19 1932 he wrote to Buck:

> I have thought much of you and the dear old days lately ... it is just fifty (!!) years since you were here & played in the orch: — what a lovely time we had, the first of many adventures. In this August weather I always live over again the holidays I had with you & the taste of *potted Ribble trout* comes with ineffaceable relish; nothing so good in eating or company has occurred to me since 1882.

Dr C W Buck's surgery.

---

[1] Letter dated January 7 1887

18

'Cravendale', Dr C W Buck's home at Giggleswick.

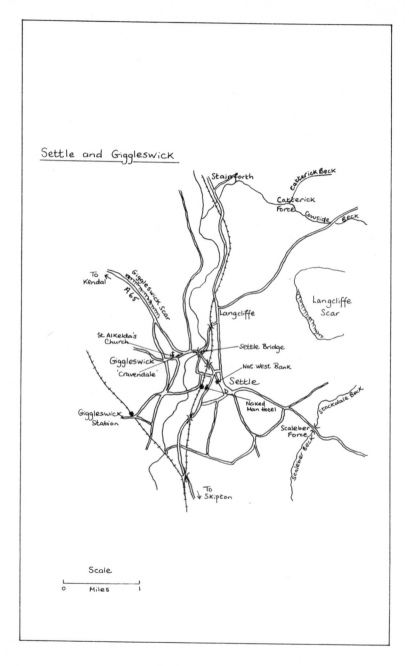

Settle and Giggleswick

Scale

0   Miles   1

In 1884 Buck married John Beare's sister, Emma. On hearing the news Elgar wrote on September 14:

> My dear doctor — I saw in the Telegraph that the event had at last come off & send my sincere congratulations ... I send you two pieces of Worcester ware, which I beg you will accept as a proof of my sincere regard.

Both Elgar and Buck were very fond of dogs. Buck had two terriers, named Potiphar and Scap. In 1885, Buck presented Scap to Elgar and thereafter Elgar's letters are full of references to Scap and his antics:

> ... There is a tripe shop between here & the High Street & Master Scap can smell the cooking of cowheels, etc.: it would do you good to see him skip into the shop & round the corner, & then fly out with the old woman after him.[1]

When he visited the Bucks later that year he took the dog with him, having assured Mrs Buck that the animal had a good moral character, liked children and had no fleas! Lucy Pipe, Elgar's sister, with whom he was living at the time, continued to look after the dog after Elgar's marriage. Scap died on September 7 1892 when Elgar was living at 'Forli'.

Buck's home at the bottom of Bell Hill in Giggleswick was called 'Cravendale'. Previously it had been a coaching-inn named the 'Hart's Head'. It had been built facing the turnpike road by the Garstang family around 1676. Robert Garstang, the last of the male line, died in 1842. His daughter Grace married Richard Hardacre Buck, a solicitor living at 'Bond End', Kirkgate, Settle. Dr Buck was their son. By 1868 the property was in the hands of Isabella Garstang, a widow, who in turn left it to her younger sister, Margaret. On her death in 1880, Dr Buck, along with his four cousins, inherited it. Later that year Buck bought them out and became the sole owner of 'Cravendale', the adjoining stables and barns and six nearby cottages, which he purchased for the sum of £760. He than moved into part of the house (now two homes called 'Cravendale' and 'Belfoot') and let the other part (now called 'Garstangs').

It is likely that Buck still lived here after his marriage, but a letter from Elgar in November 1886 suggests that the young couple had recently moved into rooms over the surgery, although the reason for this is unknown and 'Cravendale' still remained Buck's property:

---

[1] Letter dated January 8 1886

> ... I suppose you are entirely at home in your new crib now; I should
> dearly like to drop in upon you tonight as I feel lonely and uneasy &
> the idea of using 20 gallons of water (I believe that was the flush) each
> *time* would delight my prodigal soul.

Clearly, Buck had been telling Elgar of the 'facilities' installed in his
new residence. From this time on therefore, it must be assumed that
some, if not all, of Elgar's visits were to the house in Settle Market
Place.

Elgar was fascinated by the Naked Man Hotel (now a café) just
across the square and in October 1888 Elgar asked Buck, for the
second time, for a photograph of the hotel and suggested it be taken
'from my bedroom window', which supposes his room overlooked the
Market Place. Later, when Elgar attended a photographic exhibition
at the Crystal Palace, he was delighted to see that 'some enterprising
soul sent 8 or 9 photos of Settle and district, including 3 of the Market
Place, showing the N----M--Hotel, but not your house'. He adds,
'I went and glazed at 'em many times'.

On May 8 1889 Elgar married Caroline Alice Roberts at the
London Oratory. Buck made the long journey to attend the wedding
and Elgar was delighted. Later, on October 6 Elgar wrote to his friend:

> And now (after all our talks about the mystery of living) I must tell
> you how happy I am in my new life & what a dear, loving companion
> I have & how sweet everything seems & how *understandable* existence
> seems to have grown: but you may forget the long discussions we used
> to have in your carriage when driving about but I think all the difficult
> problems are now solved & — well I don't worry myself about 'em now.

The Bucks visited the Elgars the following year, shortly after the birth
of their daughter Carice Irene. Elgar also continued to visit the Bucks,
sometimes with his wife, when he had conducting engagements, for
instance at Sheffield or Leeds. The visits were usually short, exten-
ding over a few days. After a visit with Alice in 1899 Elgar wrote:

> A patch in the old year which bears thinking of with pleasure was our
> little visit to Settle.

His postscript read 'Oh! the mad days'. As Elgar's fame increased
the visits became less frequent, but the correspondence continued,
although it was a little more withdrawn. Buck, however, kept nearly
all Elgar's letters which give a remarkable insight into their friendship.

Unfortunately, Emma Buck died in 1902, leaving Buck with a son,
Morton, in his teens and a young daughter, Monica, who as a child
of six remembered sitting on Elgar's knee. For a short time Buck

ROSEMARY

('That's for Remembrance')

EDWARD ELGAR.

moved to the York area and subsequently married the daughter of the Archdeacon of York, Ella Margaret Watkins, at Whitby in 1903. He returned to his home at Giggleswick around 1906, after the early death of his second wife and when he himself retired from his practice owing to ill health.

The 'Cravendale' property is built in the shape of a square around Garstang's Yard. It is of local stone and maintains the original stone slated roof on the main building and the coach-house which stands at the rear. The house has a cellar and a large loft which was reached by narrow steps with ropes to grip. On the left-hand front bedroom window is scratched in the glass: 'This window put in by C. W. Buck 1909'. An original dresser remains in an alcove in one of the back rooms, which was probably the 'snug' of the inn.

Buck's music-room was at the back on the first floor and was approached from Garstang's Yard behind the house or by a door from the house itself. It was previously the inn's dining room and measured 21 feet by 16 feet. From the music-room there was a way through, below a dovecote, to the barn above the coaching house. Large nails were hammered into the walls where Buck hung his various stringed instruments, and there were holes in the linoleum where he placed his 'cello. The grand piano stood in one corner. In this room the Settle Orchestra was rehearsed, Buck standing in front of the fireplace to conduct. The present owner of this part of the house found a stack of music in the loft inscribed with Buck's name. The orchestra would accompany the productions of the local amateur operatic society, invariably Gilbert and Sullivan, which took place in the Victoria Hall just a few yards from the Settle — Carlisle railway. Before the days of double-glazing the passage of the many steam trains must have often distracted somewhat from the performances!

Buck also played in an amateur orchestra at Barnoldswick, was president of the Bolton Musical Artists (Society) and of the Settle Naturalist and Antiquarian Society, as well as being churchwarden of Settle Parish Church at various periods.

It is perhaps inevitable that some music resulted as a subsequence of Elgar's holidays with Buck. On his first visit, in September 1882, Elgar wrote the piece entitled *Rosemary* for piano solo and also a *Scherzo*. Regarding the latter, a violinist of the Halle Orchestra, Mr H Rigby, bought some of Buck's effects after his death, including an *Air de Ballet* copy. In reply to Rigby's letter asking for confirmation of its authenticity, Elgar wrote:

Dear Mr Rigby, *Marl Bank, Worcester, May 22, 1933.*
    The M.S. is not my writing. The little piece was published in another

form long ago. It was written in about 1876. Among my dear old friend's music there should be a Minuet (or scherzo sort of thing) for V^{n}cello and Piano which I wrote at Giggleswick in 1882 — but it's probably lost. I cannot recall anything else. I am glad you like the Concerto.

Yours sincerely,
EDWARD ELGAR.

In 1885 Elgar dedicated a *Gavotte* in A major for violin and piano to 'son ami Dr. C. W. Buck in memory of the old days.' Naturally after several holidays Elgar made the acquaintance of various other local inhabitants, including Jack Baguley of Settle, who was a close friend of Buck's. His untimely death in 1885 caused Elgar to write the song *Thro' the long days* during his August visit. It was to be Elgar's first published song, but its first public performance was not given until 12 years later. On September 15 he wrote a piano accompaniment to a piece by Buck entitled *Melody*. In a letter to Buck written on January 7 1887, Elgar refers to a Trio, apparently written by Buck, to which he adds a *Scherzo and Trio*:

> The Trio came safely to hand & we have played the slow movement several times in private & the verdict is — gigantic! It is too monstrous however for three instruments. Fiddle, 'cello & piano all seem to distend themselves frog-wise 'till they burst in a vain endeavour to represent an orchestra. Since I received it I have added a 'Scherzo & Trio', which is *jam*. The Scherzo is new & very difficult, but goes with a swing wh: would make you dance to Pen-y-Ghent & carry a cage of parrots as well (do you remember our exploit?). The Trio (mea culpa) I have transferred bodily from the little thing I wrote for you on my first visit to Giggleswyke [sic]; and I humbly ask pardon but think it too good & sugary to be left to your tender mercies only. I hope to play this with you some day.

The exploit referred to involved Buck and Elgar carrying a parrot in a cage slung on a stick between them. As they crossed Settle Bridge the bottom of the cage dropped out and they continued on their way, leaving the parrot unnoticed sitting in the road!

At the end of August 1888, most probably at Settle, Elgar wrote *Liebesgruss*, for piano solo as an engagement present for Alice.[1] He sold it outright in 1889 to Schotts for about £5, but few copies were sold and the publishers changed its name, and thereby its fortune, to *Salut d'Amour*. In 1890 Elgar arranged a local folk-song for voice and piano entitled *Clapham Town End*, presumably part of Buck's

---

[1] Their engagement was announced on September 22 1888

collection of songs. According to Elgar it was 'An old Yorkshire ballad taken down from the singing of old Tommy Kerr as he got it from his grandfather. Harmonised in strict accordance with the spirit of the age.' He also composed several 'cello obligati to popular ballads for Buck to play.

Owing to Buck's early retirement from his practice, he was thereafter able to live a quiet life and devote himself entirely to his music. In his old age he was often to be seen walking around the village in a long black cloak and wide-brimmed black hat. He died in 1932 and is buried in St Alkelda's churchyard near his home at Giggleswick. After his death the ageing Elgar wrote letters to the doctor's family which have survived and show the great sadness Elgar felt after such a prolonged and exceptional friendship.

When Buck died, 'Cravendale' was sold and split into three separate dwellings. It has been renovated inside, especially by the author John Finch, who owned the left-hand cottage, but the character of the original building was kept; externally at least it can have altered little since Buck's day.

'Hasfield Court' near Gloucester

This was the home of William Meath Baker, a country squire and a scholar who was devoted to the music of Wagner. He was a small, wiry man with a great deal of energy and an emphatic way of speaking. The Bakers were great friends of Alice. Mary Frances Baker, William's sister, had studied geology with Alice, who took her quiet and shy fiancé over to Hasfield to introduce him to the family. Despite their aristocratic background, the Bakers remained loyal to Alice after her marriage and visited the Elgars at their first home in London. The Elgars always referred to W.M.B. as 'The Squire'.

'Hasfield Court' has a beautiful setting on a small rise with formal gardens beneath it and, stretching into the distance, meadowland edged with trees. Originally the medieval court belonged to the Pauncefoot family. The oldest surviving parts of the house date from the sixteenth century and include the panelling in the former dining-room which bears the initials of Richard (d. 1588) and Dorothy Pauncefoot (d. 1568), a blocked doorway, a window at the back of the house and a central arch of the stable block. In the mid-seventeenth century the house was rebuilt as a square building, gabled on its south and west sides with a projecting west porch. There is also a seventeenth-century dovecote in the garden.

William Meath Baker's uncle bought the house from the local architect, Thomas Fulljames, in 1863 and had the exterior completely changed. The walls, which had been half brick and half stone, were re-faced entirely with stone. The gables were replaced by smaller Dutch gables surmounted by urns and linked by a balustraded parapet. Also added at this time was the neo-Renaissance porch.

In 1892 Mary Baker, or Minnie as she was called, organized a holiday to Bavaria for the Elgars, who went to stay as 'Hasfield Court' in order to discuss the arrangements. Dora Penny (Dorabella of the *Enigma Variations*), who was to become Minnie Baker's stepdaughter in 1895, gives an insight into Elgar's activities during the hot weather:

> He used to bring in hedgehogs from the woods and feed them in the house. He sat in the strawberry bed and wished that someone would bring him champagne in a bedroom jug.[1]

[1] *Memories of a Variation*, Mrs Dora M Powell, p 2

The Three Choirs Festival of 1898 was held at Gloucester and the Elgars stayed at 'Hasfield Court' with a large house-party for this and succeeding festivals held in Gloucester. Dorabella recalls in her book one particular occasion that year:

> ... a day that I particularly remember was when the whole party stay-ing there was taken over to a Point-to-Point meeting. The ladies of the party were in the library after breakfast and we heard a quick step coming along the hall. 'There's Bill', someone said, 'Now we shall get our orders for the day'. He came in, shut the door sharply behind him, and stood against it. 'Oh, here you all are! That's all right. Now, about this business today, consulting a card in his hand, 'the Brougham will take three, five can go in the brake — and someone will have to drive over with me in the dog-cart'. His eye fell on me, sitting on the floor near the large wood fire.
>
> 'Dora, will *you* come?
> 'Oh *please.*' I cried joyfully. Now that really was delightful and I knew that I was in for a jolly day.
> 'Well, look here', he went on, 'we must get over to this place by twelve sharp, and I've arranged the start for eleven-fifteen'.
>
> And he disappeared as suddenly as he had come, pulling the door behind him with a loud clap.[1]

Being rather an eccentric character he often wore his Hunt coat and knee-breeches for dinner when he had a house-party at his home. He felt it was a good way in which to wear the coats out!

One evening in 1898, some time after returning from 'Hasfield Court', Elgar was extemporizing on the piano for Alice. Enjoying the theme he was playing she asked what it was. 'Nothing', he replied, 'but something might be made of it ...' Having played a little more he asked, 'Who is that like?' 'I cannot quite say, but it is exactly the way W.M.B. goes out of the room', Alice replied with great perspi-cacity. The seed of the *Enigma Variations* had been sown and on November 1 Dorabella heard the variation entitled W.M.B. as a piano sketch, along with her own and some of the other variations. The work was orchestrated between February 5 and 19, 1899, and published later that year. It was dedicated to 'My friends pictured within'. William Meath Baker became the fourth variation, recalling the incident of William reading out the travelling arrangements he had made for his guests, delivering his message in a forceful manner before leaving the music room 'with an inadvertent bang of the door'. Bars 15—24 make suggestion of the teasing attitude of the guests.

---

[1] *Memories of a Variation*, op cit, pp 105—6

Dorabella was to become the tenth variation and William's brother-in-law, Richard Baxter Townshend, who was married to his sister Dora, the third. The variation R.B.T. also has connections with an incident at 'Hasfield Court' in about 1895 when R.B.T. played an old man in an amateur theatrical, much against his will, his usually low voice occasionally flying off into a soprano timbre. He was a likeable eccentric who rode about Oxford on a tricycle, constantly ringing his bell so that people would know he was coming, as being slightly deaf himself he was unable to hear them. Dorabella says, 'Elgar has got him with his funny voice and manner — *and* the tricycle! It is all a huge joke to anyone who knew him well.'[1]

The Bakers had three sons who, after studying various Royalist plots, acted them out, taking on the characters of Prince Rupert, the Duke of Buckingham and the Earl of Rochester. When the Elgars (along with A J Jaeger) visited the house in September 1901, Elgar himself was delighted with these 'japes'. Entering in wholeheartedly he became 'Nanty Ewart', who was the captain of the brig *Jumping Jenny* from Scott's novel *Redgauntlet*. Henceforth Elgar was always known in the Hasfield circle as 'Nanty'.

The gardens at 'Hasfield Court' had lawns sloping down to a long pool and many hidden paths among the trees, which was an ideal setting for the re-enactment of the plots. One account of these happenings which on this particular day was not resolved was recounted by one of William's sons and is recorded by Dorabella in *Memories of a Variation*:

> We boys were in the garden waiting for Nanty to come out. He had waved to us from his bedroom window so I went indoors to meet him. In the hall I saw Mrs. Elgar, a packet of letters in her hand, the afternoon post having just come. She was going to take them upstairs but as she saw Nanty coming down, she waited and held the letters out to him. 'But I'm going out now', he said, taking them from her and, with a very Nantyish oath, he threw them down on the floor and they scattered in all directions.
>
> 'Oh, Edward, that was naughty!'
>
> I picked the letters up and gave them to her. Remarking quietly 'These must be answered at once', she held them out to him. With a shout of ribald laughter he took them from her and went straight back, upstairs, without another word. I went out and told the boys that Nanty could not come just yet. We did not see him until tea time.[2]

---

[1] *Memories of a Variation*, op cit, p. 104
[2] p 102

A 'Nanty Ewart' correspondence was begun by Elgar and the three boys which continued to flourish for many months.

William Meath Baker died in 1935 and settled the estate on his second son, Francis Meath Baker. He is buried in Hasfield church-yard. When the garden at Elgar's birthplace was being laid out in 1938, prior to its opening by the Corporation of Worcester, chrysan-themums were sent from 'Hasfield Court' to be planted in the garden in memory of W.M.B.

'Hasfield Court' (south side).

Wolverhampton

Since their early days as neighbours and as students together, Alice Elgar and Mary Frances Baker (Minnie) had remained firm friends. They had studied geology together with the Reverend William Samuel Symonds, Rector of Pendock, Worcestershire, and spent many happy hours fossil-hunting on the banks of the River Severn.

On August 28 1895, Minnie became the second wife of the Reverend Alfred Penny of Wolverhampton, who on April 24 of that year had been inducted as Rector of St Peter's Collegiate Church. Dora Penny, the Rector's daughter by his first marriage, was then at the impressionable age of 21. She was intelligent, lively and musical, and greatly enthusiastic about the music of Elgar. It was to her intense delight therefore that her step-mother invited the Elgars to stay at the rectory after a performance of *The Black Knight* in Birmingham in the following December. Although it had not been a particularly good performance, Elgar's music had been acclaimed. Dora and Minnie met them at Wolverhampton Station on December 6. Alice and Minnie had naturally much to discuss and Dora was left to talk to Elgar. The two immediately became firm friends, but Dora was surprised that Elgar much preferred to talk about football than music. The prime interest of Dora's father was in the Melanesian Mission, in which he had served, and his musical appreciation was limited to a few hymns. Her friendship with the Elgars therefore was like a breath of fresh air in her stultifying existence at the rectory.

The rectory itself lay to the east of the high medieval Church of St Peter, accessible through the churchyard and standing within a walled garden. It was a large Queen Anne residence, built of small, dark red bricks, with a steep pitched roof. An uneven path from the gate led to the front door. Inside was a wood-panelled, narrow hall from which, on the right, a door led into the drawing-room which was on a slightly lower level. This room had a low ceiling and retained the original glass in the window. Down some narrow stairs at the back of the house was the stone-floored kitchen. Behind the house was a courtyard laid with red brick, with stables on the left and, directly ahead, the wall of the kitchen garden.

On entering the drawing-room, Elgar's eyes immediately fell on the piano which Minnie had brought along with several other pieces of furniture from 'Hasfield Court'. '"Hullo, there's the black piano!

Let's see how its inside has stood the move",[1] he exlaimed and settled down at once to play.' After Elgar had taken a score from his pocket, Dora began to turn the pages for him, something she was to do many times in the future, when she was to hear so much of Elgar's music long before its publication:

> It was quite straight-forward at first, but soon I noticed that other things were being put in which were not on the printed page. However, I seemed to make no mistake and in a few minutes he stopped, shut up the score and put it away. It struck me afterwards that I had been through — and seemed to have passed — a sort of examination. In later years I often remembered that day. Faced with an almost blank page of music-paper with perhaps a few pencilled notes on it, I was expected to turn over at the right time when he was playing some full orchestral passage, covering apparently the whole keyboard. I often wondered how many mistakes I made. He never scolded or laughed; he just went on, and I went on too, with great joy, hoping for the best. [2]

Later, after lunch, he discovered a high-backed chair he remembered, which was faulty, the back immediately coming off when it was moved. Asking why it hadn't been mended, Elgar asked for some tools and proceeded to carry out the repair in Dora's sitting room. 'Now understand clearly', he said, 'if this is a success *I* mended it; if it's a failure *you* did.' It was this, Dora believed, that sealed their friendship.

This was to be the first of many visits to Wolverhampton Rectory by the Elgars, who were able to explore the Staffordshire countryside and the Black Country industries with the Pennys. Dora herself was to spend many hours as a guest of the Elgars from 1896 onwards at their homes in Malvern and Hereford, and it is from her book that much of the home life of the Elgars is gleaned.

On October 17 1896, Alice and Edward returned to the rectory for a long weekend. Elgar had a choral rehearsal in Stoke that evening in preparation for a performance of *King Olaf*, which had been commissioned for the Hanley Festival a fortnight later, on October 30. The performance in the Victoria Hall, Hanley, was to be a great success, but on the afternoon of the 17th, Elgar's thoughts seemed far away from his music. He and Dora visited the football match to see the Wolves Reserves beat Singers' FC 4 – 0 in a Birmingham League match. Elgar was a great fan of Wolves and enjoyed every minute:

---

[1] *Memories of a Variation*, op cit, p 3

[2] *Edward Elgar: Centenary Sketches. The Music Maker*, Mrs Dora M Powell, pp 33 – 34

It all delighted him. The dense crowd flowing down the road like a river; the roar of welcome as the rival teams came on to the ground; the shouts of men calling to their player-friends by their Christian names — usually considerably shortened; the staccato 'Aw!' at a mishap (a most remarkable sound from a crowd of sixty thousand); and the deafening roar that greeted a goal. He was much taken with the names of some of the players — particularly Malpas, a famous member of the Wolves at that time. I have known him say when we met:

'There you are. How's Malpas? — a question I was not always able to answer.'[1]

For Malpas, the centre-half, Elgar composed a *leitmotiv* which was to become the property of Dora. The rehearsal that evening went well and Elgar returned to the rectory full of all that had happened. The following day he spent nearly the whole time on the piano playing over parts of *King Olaf* and other pieces, much to Dora's great delight.

In July 1897 the Elgars again visited the rectory and this time stayed for five days. Shortly after lunch one day Dora took Elgar by tram to the Dunstall Park race-course, where friends of hers had given her permission to take any visitors to see the racing. They managed to see three races and then joined the others at the gates to pay a visit to the nearby Boscobel House. As they got into the carriage Elgar remarked, 'This is what I call eating one's cake and having it'. Boscobel House is a Jacobean farmhouse with a beautiful seventeenth-century lavender garden. Here, in a secret priest's hole upstairs, Charles II hid after the Battle of Worcester, having spent some time previously hiding in an oak tree in the grounds. Elgar was fascinated with the house and went all over it; he was also able to indulge in his new hobby of kite-flying in the fields outside. On this visit Dora was treated to a great deal of music, including *The Light of Life*, sketches from *Caractacus* and *From the Bavarian Highlands*. Dora particularly liked the *Lullaby (Near Hammersbach)* and asked to dance to it. Elgar was so pleased by this that later, during her visits to Malvern, she was often called upon to 'come and dance *Hammersbach*'.

During February 1898 the Elgars stayed at Wolverhampton for nearly a week, during which time *King Olaf* was produced at Birmingham and at Wolverhampton. Another football match was attended and afterwards Dora had to send Elgar a copy of the local newspaper containing an account of the match. The reporter had used the words 'he banged the leather for goal', which so delighted Elgar

---

[1] *Memories of a Variation*, op cit, p4

that he set the words to music. In the letter replying to Dora's he continues:

> I have a mug — not the one with the moustache, which you have seen (and heard) — but a brand new one, to drink out of, made at Hanley & presented to me with my name & an extract from K. Olaf.[1]

In 1899, to relieve Alice of the responsibility, Dora took on a position as 'Keeper of the Archives', a task on which she devoted many hours for almost fifteen years; sorting, cataloguing and mounting all the newspaper reviews of performances of Elgar's music. That same year she was to become the tenth variation in the *Enigma* portrayals, her movement, according to Elgar, suggesting 'a dancelike lightness'. Dora discovered years later that Elgar had parodied her stammer. Elgar's nickname 'Dorabella', which he had adopted early in their relationship and which gives the title to the piece, is a pseudonym adopted from Mozart's *Cosi fan tutti*. Elgar wrote to Dora on February 22: 'The Variations are finished & yours is the most cheerful ... I *have* orchestrated you well.' She remained a firm friend and loyal assistant for many years, cycling some 40 miles from Wolverhampton to Malvern on many occasions, often to spend time trying to cheer Elgar or understand his erratic moods.

Dora's time was taken up at home by helping with the various activities of the parish, such as bazaars, sales, entertainments and the inevitable committee meetings. She also ran her own string orchestra for four years and for 18 seasons sang in the Wolverhampton Choral Society. Whenever she made any slight criticism of Elgar's music he would retort: 'What do you know about it? You're only a Chorus Girl!'

In January 1900, Elgar visited Wolverhampton again in order to attend another football match. He had wanted to go to the Wolverhampton Festival held in the summer of 1902 but in the end did not attend, although Alice and Carice went on July 25.

The Wolverhampton Choral Society decided to perform *The Dream of Gerontius* in 1904. Much to Dora's horror the concert was to take place during Lent, when, due to her family's strict observance, no concerts were allowed — only sacred music, usually performed in church. Dora's father had attended a performance of *Gerontius* in Birmingham and had been bored. Earlier, in 1900, when Dora had returned from a trip to Malvern and had played and sung part of 'Praise to the Holiest', the Reverend Penny had said: 'But *surely* he is going to use the fine tune in Ancient and Modern? He'll be making

---

[1] *Memories of a Variation*, op cit, p 4

a terrible mistake if he doesn't.' When invited to sing in the semi-chorus at the 1904 performance, Dora had to tackle her father with the request to take part. The following conversation, recorded by Dora in *Memories of a Variation*, followed:

> You know quite well we don't go to musical entertainments in Lent?'
> 'But this is sacred music'.
> 'Is it?'
> 'The words are sacred'.
> 'Some of them may be. But it is called a "Dream"; I should call it a nightmare, but it isn't true — which is one mercy. Do you call that *sacred*?'
> 'If it was the "*Messiah*" you wouldn't mind my singing it even though it was not in church?'
> 'Now you are not going to pretend that *the Dream of Gerontius* by your friend Dr. Elgar is on a par with the *Messiah*?'[1]

Although she was allowed to sing in the rehearsals, it was not in the semi-chorus. The most difficult thing for Dora was to write and explain the matter to the Elgars.

On October 16 1907 the Elgars went to tea at the rectory after the rehearsal of a concert to be held at Birmingham that evening, when the two families talked endlessly and heard a good deal of music. In the July of 1909, Carice went to stay with the Penny's for the annual floral fete, greatly enjoying the flowers, bands and fireworks. Meetings between the families became less frequent, however, especially when the Elgars moved to 'Severn House' in Hampstead. In January 1913, Dora married Richard C Powell, and although she took her husband to London in the following spring to meet the Elgars, it was only through the fact that she remained 'Keeper of the Archives' that any contact continued after that.

Dora's father continued to serve as Rector of Wolverhampton until 1919. In 1935 the rectory was purchased by Wolverhampton Council and used as civic offices. Outbuildings were added to it and it still remains as a block of offices to the present day.

---

[1] p 58

Chelsea and Tintagel

In 1897 Elgar met Alice Sophia Caroline Stuart-Wortley, the daughter of the artist Sir John Millais. She was the second wife of Charles Stuart-Wortley, the Conservative MP for the Hallam division of Sheffield. A keen amateur pianist, she adored Elgar's music and always responded sensitively to it. Elgar was 40 when they met and she was 35. At first their relationship was fairly formal but became less so about 1906. Elgar's letters to her always show the greatest affection and it is to her that he often expresses his most intimate thoughts. She in her turn appears to have had a great influence on him and his music.

The first performance of Elgar's *Coronation Ode*, with words by A C Benson, was given at Sheffield in 1902. On this occasion the Elgars were looked after by the Stuart-Wortleys. The two families had been introduced by Lady Alice Fitzwilliam, with whom the Elgars lunched one day during their visit. Elgar, however, was 'not pleased with the company or food & excused himself & went off'. He was in agony with acute toothache, and after suffering for two days had it extracted and therefore had to conduct *Gerontius* whilst still under the influence of the gas.

The London home of the Stuart-Wortleys was at 7, Cheyne Walk, Chelsea, and the Elgars often visited them here. It is a large red-brick house consisting of five floors and a basement and stands off the Chelsea Embankment, opposite the Albert Bridge. Set in the garden wall is a Victorian pillar box which Alice Stuart-Wortley must have used to send her many letters to Elgar. The two families seem to have enjoyed each other's company. Alice Elgar often wrote letters in an affectionate manner to 'my dearest namesake' and Elgar was to give some early sketches of the *Violin Concerto* to Charles. Nevertheless, Alice Stuart-Wortley and Elgar appear to have had a certain rapport which brought them very close in musical thought and feeling. They had much in common: both loved the countryside and both hated the cold. Their letters to each other are littered with statements about the weather. Elgar was very fond of Pre-Raphaelite school of painters, of which Alice's father was one of the chief exponents.

In 1909 Elgar wrote the part-song *Angelus (Tuscany)* in Italy and dedicated it to Mrs Charles Stuart-Wortley. She may have been the 'soul' enshrined in the *Violin Concerto* of 1910 and inspired parts of the *Second Symphony*. Although Dorabella states categorically that the 'soul' was Julia Worthington, Elgar always referred to 'our own concerto' and 'your symphony' when writing to Alice. He called her 'Windflower' and on April 27 1910, whilst composing the *Violin Concerto*, he wrote:

> I have been working hard at the windflower themes — but all stands still until you come and approve.

The following day he wrote to her again:

> The tunes stick and are not windflowerish — at present.

Earlier that month Elgar had been on a motoring tour of Cornwall and Devon with Frank Schuster. The Stuart-Wortleys owned land at Tintagel, and the family had built the Wharncliffe Arms Hotel, but it appears that in the first instance the itinerary was going to avoid a visit there. Elgar wrote to Alice from Torquay, where they had been since March 30:

> I am with Frank and his sister and tomorrow commence a motor tour 'round' Cornwall avoiding Tintagel, it seems, but I am not *director* or dictator or Heaven knows what wd. happen to you or to Tintagel ... Love, Windflower, Yours E.[1]

However, an alteration in the proposed route must have been made, for the diary reads:

> Torquay, Plymouth (April 2)
> Tintagel (April 3)
> Penzance, Truro, Land's End (April 4)
> Falmouth (April 6)
> Fowey (April 7)
> Exeter (April 8)
> Salisbury, Stonehenge (April 9)
> Winchester (April 10)

They had glorious sunshine but rather cold easterly winds. Elgar was delighted to find rhododendrons and camellias in full bloom and was amazed at the palm trees.

The following year Elgar refers to this visit to Tintagel in a letter to Alice Stuart-Wortley from Cincinnati:

> It is sweet to hear of Tintagel & our own land ... I have lovely things to think of & shall soon be back & hope to see you. All I can do is count the days ... it is so raw & silly out here ... I am sure you are better in Tintagel — I am selfish enough to be thankful that you can think of me there & you will not forget Frank's car taking us to Boscastle & you will not forget the road home — how lovely it was — a year ago.[2]

---

[1] April 1 1910   [2] *Portrait of Elgar*, op cit, pp 236–7

The full manuscript score of the *Second Symphony* bears the following names: 'Venice — Tintagel'.

Elgar always enjoyed hearing Alice Stuart-Wortley play the piano and she often played through his works for him. Writing to her in 1911 he says:

> I do not like the piano solo players' playing but I love yours — and you will understand the difference.

She often came to 'Severn House' (which she had found for them in the summer of 1911) to play over fragments of a piano concerto. Had this concerto ever been completed he would have dedicated it to her, for when writing *The Sanguine Fan* ballet music in February 1917 he wrote:

> I thought of using *your piano concerto*! (Labour exchange!) but you would not allow that would you ... Where are you? I wanted to tell you that the theme and every note must be approved by you (bless you!) before anything can be done. Oh! Why are you so far away and so difficult to get at??

In December 1916 her husband Charles was created a peer and became Lord Stuart of Wortley. Elgar wrote to Alice on December 20 after receiving news of the peerage:

> I am out of bed and I use the first minute to send you love & congratulations on the event — I gave you a coronet long ago — the best I had but you may have forgotten it — now you will have a real one, bless you! ... I feel afraid of you & wonder in a vague sort of way what will be the difference? But you are still the windflower I think & hope.

The following year Elgar felt that his life was particularly bleak. In the spring and summer months he longed for his native Worcestershire, especially as Alice Stuart-Wortley wrote to say that she had been visiting some of Elgar's old haunts. In the spring of 1918 she visited the Elgars at 'Brinkwells', their cottage in Sussex. Before she arrived in May he wrote to her:

> The woods are still carpeted with bluebells but the heavy rain of three days ago tried them severely and they look rather faded; I have been down the wood & told them you are coming & asked them to remain for your loved visit.

In the late summer of that year she broke her leg at Tintagel and he sent her some sketches of the *Violin Sonata*.

Lord Stuart of Wortley died on April 24 1926, two days before Elgar was due to conduct the *Enigma Variations* and the *First Sym-*

phony with the London Symphony Orchestra. Elgar wrote to Alice after the concert:

> It was a great ordeal & I missed something too great to express — I looked at the familiar seats & my eyes filled.

A note with his Christmas card of 1929 said that his card 'brings my love or rather a remembrance of it since 1897 — thirty-two years' accumulation'. Each spring, to which they both looked forward, he unfailingly gathered the first windflowers to send to her — his own 'Windflower'.

7 Cheyne Walk, Chelsea —
home of Lady Alice Stuart-Wortley.

Bishop Auckland, County Durham

In 1897 the first performance of *King Olaf* was given on April 3 at the Crystal Palace. On April 27 it was produced at Bishop Auckland by Nicholas Kilburn, an amateur musician and conductor of the Bishop Auckland Music Society. A pump manufacturer by profession, he had an overwhelming enthusiasm for Elgar's music. After this performance he was to become one of Elgar's greatest friends, conducting many of his works and travelling to the Leeds Festivals and the Three Choirs Festivals in order to hear Elgar's music performed. When in 1901 Elgar became a Doctor of Music, Kilburn was one of the subscribers to the Cambridge robes which Elgar could not afford to pay for himself. When Kilburn heard *The Apostles* in 1903 he described it to Alice as having 'cosmic, Gerontius appeal'.

On June 21 1904 an honorary Doctorate of Music was conferred on Elgar by the University of Durham. After the ceremony he stayed for the night with the Kilburns at 'Ninefields', Bishop Auckland, as he often did when visiting the north. He left on June 22, returning home to find that Alice had placed an important letter in the safe; the King had made him a Knight. During the Leeds Festival of that year, apart from the performance of *In the South*, Alice particularly enjoyed seeing the Kilburns.

For the Three Choirs Festival of 1909, held at Hereford, the Elgars had intended to hold a large house-party at their home, 'Plas Gwyn'. Unfortunately, Carice contracted scarlet fever, so Elgar hired Harley House in Hereford in order to entertain his friends. Among the guests were the Kilburns. As part of the revelry Elgar made out a programme for a private concert to be held at the house. Included in the orchestral section were:

Percussion	Mrs Worthington & Mr N Kilburn
Principal Solo Bagpipe	Mrs N Kilburn

After writing to Elgar on November 4 1910, Kilburn added a postscript asking what the words inscribed on the *Violin Concerto* meant. By return of post Elgar replied:

> Aqui esta encerranda el alma de ... Here, or more emphatically *in here,* is enshrined or simply enclosed — burial is perhaps too definite — *the soul of* ...? The final 'de' leaves it indefinite as to sex or rather gender. Now guess.

40

Elgar never revealed to him his secret — another enigma![1]

In 1899, when Elgar had been working on the *Enigma Variations*, a sketch which he had not used had been headed 'Kilburn'. However, in 1912 he dedicated *The Music Makers*, with words by Arthur O'Shaughnessy, to Nicholas Kilburn. The work was composed over several years; he probably started work on it about 1903 and much of it was sketched at Mordiford Bridge, one of Elgar's favourite spots. Kilburn had been associated with all Elgar's great works, many of which are recalled in this work. There are quotations from the *Variations, Gerontius* and the *Violin Concerto*, and this may explain the reason for Elgar writing the work in this way. Dr Percy Young writes:

> So Elgar, back to the intimate, cryptic manner, recommends his own first choices to his friend, and attaches, by verbal label, additional significance to particular phrases.[2]

Elgar himself thought he had written a good work — 'good (enough for me)', he wrote.

The first performance was given at the Birmingham Festival on October 1 1912. Shortly afterwards it was produced by Kilburn in Sunderland. After rehearsing the work, Kilburn wrote to Lady Elgar on December 24:

> I have desired to tell him and you that my Choral folk love the Music Makers. All three Choirs alike who have now tasted it. The strong virility and charm of the music appeals to them, and the interest is manifestly sincere and alive. 'Tis delightful to find difficulties which do not dismay, but give zest; stimulating even the stodgiest! Whole tone scale, the obliquely intertwined tune, and the quotations, all a quaintness and a delight. With what genuine fitness of feeling dear 'Gerontius' themes here take their place.

Kilburn obviously thoroughly understood the work and the poetical choral writing. He knew exactly what to ask his choirs to produce. After the performance he wrote:

> Especially did I strive to impress on all concerned the importance of a subdued mystical treatment of certain parts of the words. Sing and play, I said, as though you were in *dreamland* then all will be well.

At the end of the work, after the words 'the dreamer slumbers and the singer sings no more', there is a quotation from *Gerontius* — 'novissima hora', also present in the *Minuet* for pianoforte which in

---

[1] See p 36
[2] *Elgar O.M.*, Percy Young, p 303

1897 Elgar had written for Kilburn's son Paul, who was a composer and a member of the Scottish National Orchestra.[1]

The following year *Falstaff* was given its first London performance, at the Albert Hall on December 14. Kilburn was present and enthused greatly about the work to Lady Elgar afterwards. He himself continued to perform works into his seventies. From December 1–4 1919, although Lady Elgar was ill at the time and unable to attend, Elgar went again to Bishop Auckland to conduct for Kilburn there and at Middlesbrough. The concert held on December 2 at Bishop Auckland was good, but the *Enigma Variations* had to be played without rehearsal as the orchestra had turned up one and a half hours late.

Kilburn died at the beginning of 1924, aged 80 — one of Elgar's oldest and dearest friends and a great champion of his music.

---

[1] Paul died in 1957

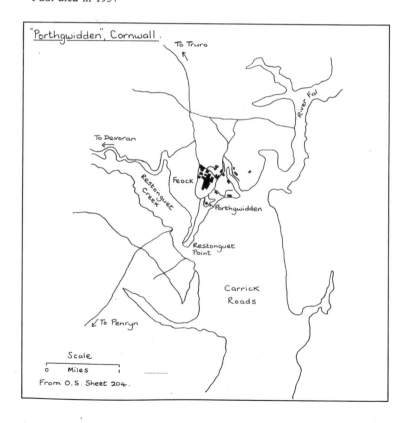

'Porthgwidden', Feock, Devoran, Cornwall

Lady Mary Lygon, inaugurator of the Madresfield Festival at Malvern, where many of Elgar's works were performed and which he conducted himself, became a great friend of the Elgar family. 'Madresfield Court', the Tudor mansion of the Beauchamp family, is situated on the western side of the River Severn to the north-east of the Malvern Hills. Elgar's father had often visited Madresfield as its piano tuner, little realising that his son would regularly become a guest at the house. Lady Mary was the sister of Lord Beauchamp, Governor of New South Wales from 1899 to 1901, and she accompanied her brother to Australia in 1899. At the same time she was to become immortalised as the thirteenth variation in *Enigma*. Elgar marked the variation with three asterisks, for by the publication date she had already sailed. Dorabella says that they stood for 'My Sweet Mary'. The throb of the ship's engines can be clearly discerned in the music and above this is a quotation from Mendelssohn's overture *Calm Sea and a Prosperous Voyage*. Published in the same year but before the *Enigma Variations*, Elgar had dedicated his *Three Characteristic Pieces* to Lady Mary Lygon. They had been written between 1882 and 1888, but were revised by Elgar in 1899 and are: No. 1, *Mazurka; No. 2, Serenade Mauresque*; No. 3, *Contrasts: The Gavotte A.D. 1700 and 1900.*

In 1905, Lady Mary married Major the Honourable Henry William Hepburn-Stuart-Forbes Trefusis, JP, who had a home called 'Porthgwidden'' near the tiny village of Feock in Cornwall. The handsome mid-nineteenth-century residence stands near the church. It is surrounded by 20 acres of ground, which include private gardens and golf links, running down to Restonguet Creek.

On July 2 1910 the Elgars went down to Cornwall to stay at 'Porthgwidden', as Elgar had been overworking and needed a rest. He travelled from London and met Alice at Bristol. He was obviously delighted by the surroundings and the golf, but appeared to find the society company a little restrictive. From here he wrote to his friend and patron Frank Schuster:

MY DEAR FRANKIE,
It is heavenly etc. here! but I would like to choose my company as

43

you allow us (me?) to do at the Hut. You remember we looked round the corner of the House on to the terrace.[1] Lady M. is of old & always very 'nice' & dear & rather severe. Of the rest I will tell you. Alice is radiantly happy & sleeps always — the air is divinely resposeful.

You would love this garden of 'nooks' & corners & the sea.

I wish you and

...! and

...!! and

...!!! were here.

... Now I am sleepy again — cream I suppose.

    Love,

      Yrs. ever

        EDWARD.[2]

During the week they took a motor boat to St Just in Roseland and another down the River Fal and also had a trip to Truro. They left on July 7, Elgar travelling to Bournemouth for a concert before returning home on the 9th.

This may have been the only holiday the Elgar's spent here. Alice especially, however, was pleased to be able to move in such aristocratic circles. By 1910 Lady Mary's husband had become a Lieutenant Colonel. She herself had been Woman of the Bedchamber to the Princess of Wales since 1895 and so in 1912, when Alice needed someone to present her at court, it was Lady Trefusis who offered her services.

---

[1] On April 6 that year Elgar had visited the area on a motoring tour with Schuster. See p 37

[2] Letter dated July 4 1910

Westminster and 'The Hut', Bray on Thames

Elgar's first reference to Leo Francis Schuster, or Frank as he was always known, is on May 11 1899, although they had obviously met previously, when he went to an 'at home' at Schuster's town house at 22, Old Queen Street, near St James's Park, in Westminster. Schuster came from a wealthy banking family and was a great patron of the arts. He was to become one of Elgar's closest and most generous friends for nearly 30 years. Schuster opened his homes to artists, musicians and those in literary circles. He poured a good deal of his money into music and came to have a special regard for Elgar's.

His Westminster home is of three storeys, with a basement and an attic storey with dormer windows in the roof. It is of red brick with the ground floor stuccoed to give a panelled effect. It has an imposing portico with fluted columns, and a room over the balconied porch with a balustraded frontage. On the ground floor there is a large bow-fronted room where presumably the concerts, frequently held here, were given. Elgar's *String Quartet* and *Pianoforte Quintet* were played here for the first time at an invitation concert on May 3 1919. Unfortunately, later in life Schuster suffered financially and in 1923 found it necessary to sell this beautiful house. It is at present the headquarters of an insurance company.

Schuster's other home was at Bray on Thames near Maidenhead. The village is set on a bend of the river and has fascinating irregular streets with delightful timber-framed and Georgian houses. Schuster's home, known as 'The Hut', is some way out of the village on the river side, next to the small bridge over to Monkey Island. Wooden steps lead up from the river to the house, which is raised in case of flooding. The back of the house is 150 years old and is constructed of solid timbers 15 inches thick. The front portion and the chimneys are mock Tudor and were added in 1896. The lounge at the river end was built in the shape of a cross and was added at the beginning of the twentieth century. A 20-foot-high fence of iron uprights and railway sleepers surrounded the large garden in Schuster's day, thus ensuring privacy. The owner before Schuster was Miss Van de Weyre, lady-in-waiting to Queen Victoria. The Queen often paid a visit to the house.

Across the lawn, and almost screened by trees from the house, was

22 Old Queen Street, Westminster — town house of Frank Schuster.

a music room, approached by stepping stones placed in the grass. It was a large wooden building with a stage, rather barn-like in appearance; it housed a great many curios, including Chinese ornaments, which Schuster had collected from all over the world. There were two large bay windows to the main room and also a kitchen and living quarters for the staff. It was demolished in 1959 and a modern house, called 'The Music Room', was built on the site in 1963.

There was always a large party of interesting people at 'The Hut', all going their own ways and meeting for meals on the verandah. Gabriel Fauré was a frequent visitor and composed many of his songs here. It was not long before the Elgars were invited and for many years Elgar was to enjoy numerous hours of relaxation here, going for walks by the river or on fishing expeditions. In these peaceful surroundings he received inspiration for the many compositions on which he subsequently worked. His visits to 'The Hut' appear to have become a means of escape from the burden of daily life.

After composing the overture *In the South* at Alassio in North Italy in the winter of 1903–4, Elgar dedicated it to his friend. 'F's own overture', he called it after his death: 'warm and joyous with a grave radiating serenity'.

During the Elgar Festival of 1904, Schuster gave a dinner party to honour his friend. Henry J Wood has described in his book[1] Elgar's seemingly indifferent attitude at the party; yet apparently it had been a great struggle for Elgar to attend at all, having been too ill to get up that morning with a severe headache. Only after dosing himself with various medicinal remedies did he manage to attend the function. Alice recorded in her diary[2] 'what a wonderful time it had been and how Frank had proposed E's health in a most touching way with his heart in his voice'.

Early in 1905 the Elgars visited 'The Hut' and were delighted to find that their room had been redecorated. In Schuster's music room they held a private rehearsal of the *Introduction and Allegro for String Orchestra* on which Elgar had been working for the previous two months. The following year Elgar spent nearly the whole month of July here, when, encouraged by Schuster, he put in an enormous amount of work on *The Kingdom*. Again in June 1908 he worked on his *First Symphony* at 'The Hut', once more greatly encouraged by his friend's enthusiasm. Sometimes he would work in the cross-shaped lounge, where there was a grand piano, but more often than

---

[1] *My Life and Music*, p 179
[2] March 13 1904

not he isolated himself in the music room.

One visit to Bray that is particularly well documented was his visit in 1910 with W H Reed, leader of the London Symphony Orchestra, when Elgar sketched a good deal of the *Violin Concerto*, especially the slow movement. In his book *Elgar As I knew Him*, Reed makes the following comments about one of the curios in the music room where the two were working:

> I remember particularly well a stuffed lizard, or member of that genus — a fine specimen, though perhaps rather large for a lizard. It was suspended from the ceiling in such a way as to be swayed by every gust of wind coming in through the door or window, and I always felt that it swung round to have a good look at us when we played the slow movement or the opening of the Finale, for it was here that this first took shape.[1]

Reed thought that the slow movement reflected the surroundings of the house by the Thames:

> As I saw it in that early spring, with all the young green on the trees and the swans lazily floating by on the river, so the vision comes to me again with the music that was written there, music that depicts with such fidelity the poetry and beauty of the scene.[2]

Frontage of 'The Hut'. The central doorway with the porch was then the main entrance: The house on the left is still named 'The Long White Cloud'.

---

[1] p 27   [2] *Portrait of Elgar*, op cit, p 231

'The Hut' (riverside view)

Elgar himself wrote of the ending of the work to Alice Stuart-Wortley on June 16:

> I have made the end serious & grand I hope & have brought in the real inspired themes from the 1st movement. Frank approves. I did it this morning ... the music sings of memories & hope.

The *Violin Concerto* was finished by August and on the Sunday preceeding the Three Choirs Festival at Gloucester, Schuster organised a private party, at a house known as the Cookery School on College Green, which Elgar had taken for the festival. Reed, with Elgar at the piano, played the concerto to the private audience in a large upstairs room which contained a grand piano. The evening before the first public performance on November 10 at the Queen's Hall, Schuster arranged another of his generous parties for Elgar, presumably at his town house.

In June 1912 it was *The Music Makers* that Elgar worked on at 'The Hut' and the following summer he was there again working on *Falstaff*. When the war intervened, Schuster allowed his home to be used by the military for the wounded. Elgar joined the Special Constabulary on August 17 1914 and almost immediately was promoted to Staff Inspector. He wrote the following letter in reply to a letter from Schuster asking him to visit Bray:

SPECIAL CONSTABULARY

Hampstead Station   Division
Staff Inspector   Sept. 13, 1914

Sir,

    I have to acknowledge the receipt of your letter of the 9th inst., in which you ask that a Special Constable shall be detailed to visit The Hut for an indefinite period. I must point out that it is necessary to receive fuller particulars than those contained in your letter; I shall therefore be obliged if you will give replies for the following questions as soon as convenient.

(1) For how long is the presence of the Special Constable desired?

(2) For what emergency, if any, is a special guard required?

(3) Failing the Constable asked for (Elgar, 0015014 — who is now Staff Inspector to the Division) would an ordinary policeman be equally welcome???!!!???!!!

(4) State any circumstances known to you personally which may lead the council to decide that the Hut is more important than other private dwellings and should have the special guard desired.

(5) State what feminine society The Hut will provide for No. 0015014.

On receiving your reply the matter shall be proceeded with at once.
I have the honour to be,
        Your obedient servant,
            EDWARD ELGAR
            Staff Inspector

Leo F. Schuster, Esq.,
The Hut,
Bray,
Berks.

At the end of October 1918, Elgar was at 'The Hut' with the pianist Irene Scharrer, who was shown his sketches for a piano concerto. He asked her to play them and, after hearing her, gave her the promise of a first performance, which was never to materialise as the work remained incomplete. In June 1919 he was there again, working on the *Cello Concerto*.

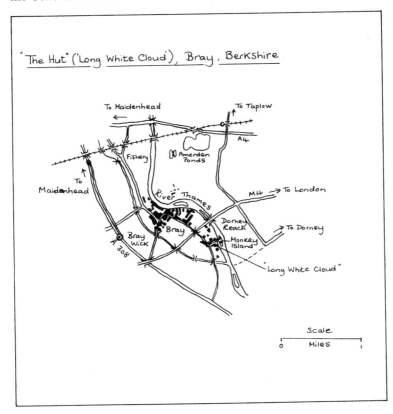

*Extract from the Violin Concerto
(reduction for violin and piano).*

That Schuster was one of Elgar's greatest admirers is unquestionable. Once during the war, after sustaining the death of a friend, he wrote to Elgar: 'I wonder if you realise when you feel despondent & embittered what your music is to me — and therefore to countless others?' Yet to Elgar after the war years, and after the death of his wife in 1920, nothing seemed the same. Even the atmosphere at 'The Hut', which had previously proved so relaxing and yet so mercurial, appeared to have changed. Writing to Alice Stuart-Wortley after a visit in October 1922, when he disapproved of some of the guests, he says:

> You cd. not say the one word to F. as usual. I tried to write but the effect has been that all idea of composition is 'choked off' so we will forget my little delusion about taking up music again: that is over.

The following year he paid another, equally disastrous, visit, again enjoying neither the holiday nor the company.

Nevertheless in 1927, during Elgar's seventieth year, as a birthday concert and as a tribute to his friend, Schuster generously arranged performances of the three chambers works as 'The Hut', which by then had been re-named 'Long White Cloud'. This new name, suggested by a New Zealand commissioner who visited here, was written on the gate and was the English form of the Maori name for New Zealand. When the Tahitians first discovered the North Island of New Zealand they saw it as a long white cloud and named it Aoteatoa. W H Reed and Albert Sammons were among those who played at the performances on June 26. Among those present were William Walton, Arnold Bennett, Siegfried Sassoon and Osbert Sitwell. Yet even after this great kindness Elgar could not be reconciled to the changes that had taken place. Alice Stuart-Wortley had been unable to be present and afterwards he wrote to her:

> You were sadly missed last Sunday at The Hut — or rather at the new place as the Hut atmosphere has gone never to return. Dear old Frank was radiant &, as usual, a perfect host ... I *hope* I behaved as becomes an old visitor.

Exactly six months later, on December 26, Frank Schuster died. His death was to prove a great blow to Elgar. Writing to Schuster's sister Adela early the next month he says: 'He was always the most loving, strongest & wisest friend man ever had. I seem dazed — to have lost a limb, to have grown older suddenly,' but to Alice Stuart-Wortley he poured out the truth of his feelings and perhaps his guilt:

> It is a dispensation of whoever controls us that in remembering childish holidays we recollect only the fine days — the bad ones do not come

back so easily; in the passing of friends it is somewhat the same: the radiant happy & sunny Frank I have before me as I write & the small temporary little irritations which worried me at the time are gone for ever.[1]

Schuster's final benevolent act was to leave Elgar £7,000 in his will, for saving England from the reproach of having produced no composer 'worthy to rank with the great masters'. His house at Bray was eventually divided into three homes, now named 'The Long White Cloud' (the river-side house), 'River Court' (which has the main front door of Schuster's home) and 'Sundial Cottage'.

---

[1] *Portrait of Elgar*, op cit, p 308

Liverpool, Saughall and Bettwys-y-Coed

Alfred E Rodewald — 'dear Rodey', as Alice referred to him — became one of Elgar's dearest friends. They had probably met on July 16 1899 at New Brighton during an Elgar concert arranged by Granville Bantock. Elgar stayed with Bantock at his home, 'Holly Mount', 19 Holland Road, Liscard. At the concert, among other works, the first performance of Elgar's *Minuet* Opus 21 was given. Rodewald was born in Liverpool but was of German descent. He was educated at Charterhouse and became a wealthy cotton magnate but he lived for his music. He was a great friend of Richter, conductor of the Hallé Orchestra, and sometimes played the double bass for him. Apart from this he conducted the largely amateur Liverpool Orchestral Society, which he raised to a high standard.

Whenever Elgar visited Liverpool for performances of his works he would stay with Rodewald at his house at 66 Huskisson Street. The terraced red-bricked house, with three storeys and a basement, dates from the early nineteenth century. In Rodewald's day there were bay windows on the ground and first floors, to the left of the front door. Two steps led to the porch, with its pillars on either side supporting impressive Ionic capitals. The house, in an elevated position close to the Anglican Cathedral, was then situated in an influential area. Now, only part of the facade of the house is original; many others in the street are derelict and awaiting redevelopment.

Rodewald also had another home, at Saughall near Chester. Known as 'The Cottage', and with a lovely garden, it was rather more than its name suggests. Earlier it had belonged to the church and it is again now The Vicarage. His summer cottage, called 'Minafon', was at Bettwys-y-Coed in Wales and the Elgars spent a fortnight there with Rodewald from June 8–17 1901. Obviously much fascinated by the country, he wrote to Troyte Griffith on June 12:

> P.S. Llanrwist-tal-y-cafn eglwsbach trefin pentrevoelas. (Don't tell anybody) I'm learning the langwidge.

On October 19 1901, Rodewald gave the first performance of the first two *Pomp and Circumstances* Marches. Elgar had dedicated No. 1 to Rodewald and the Liverpool Orchestral Society. The two men often corresponded and Rodewald's letters are always humorous

66 Huskisson Street, Liverpool,
showing original frontage.

and light-hearted, usually beginning 'Dear old cocky'. He had a genuine love of Elgar's music and after hearing Richter conduct *Cockaigne* at Manchester in 1901 he had written: 'Ah! my dear boy, you write from the heart and not the brain, there's the secret'. On 8 November he travelled to Malvern to tell Elgar that his friends had clubbed together to buy him his Cambridge doctorate robes which Elgar had said he could not afford. It was in fact Rodewald who had organized the collection.

The following year Rodewald attended the second Düsseldorf performance of *The Dream of Gerontius* on May 19. On August 8 the Elgars went to stay at Saughall for a break. Elgar took his bicycle, but it was pouring with rain when they arrived. Mr and Mrs Ernest Newman and Granville Bantock were also staying there. On August 10 Bantock conducted Elgar's *Serenade for Strings* at New Brighton and on the following day they had a trip to Chester. Soon after 10 am on August 21, Elgar left to ride home on his bicycle, Alice and Carice leaving by train at 2 pm. He slept that night at Shrewsbury. The next day he continued his journey as far as Ludlow and then caught the train to Hereford before continuing on his bicycle to Malvern. Unfortunately, he missed his way out of Ledbury, which made him late and tired, but he arrived home safe and well. Quite a feat! He had

Alfred Rodewald at his home at Bettwys-y-Coed.

to be back in Malvern by August 22 for a rehearsal of the Worcester semi-chorus for a performance of *Gerontius* on the 26th. At the end of 1902 Elgar was in Liverpool again. Here he wrote *O Sacrum Convivium*, which was planned for part three of *The Apostles* but was eventually incorporated into *The Kingdom*. The arrangement is dated '66, Huskisson Street, Liverpool, Dec. 1st 1902.'

From July 3–31 1903 the Elgars visited Rodewald at 'Minafon' in Bettwys-y-Coed. Elgar spent a good deal of the time orchestrating *The Apostles* and writing several letters to Canon Charles V. Gorton regarding the libretto. Nevertheless, he was able to see a large part of North Wales in Rodewald's car or by bicycle. On July 6 he wrote to his great friend A J Jaeger of Novellos:

> Rodewald asks you to *come here* as soon as you can and as long as you can — bring your bike & we'll do analysis ... Tell the firm it's necessary for you to come.

Jaeger replied two days later to say that although he would like to accept the invitation he could not afford it. On the 9th Elgar wrote again:

> Now: you *must* come up on Saturday — it shall *cost you nothing*.
>   It is quite free & easy here — you dress as you like & do exactly what you please — no formality or any nonsense.

This renewed invitation persuaded Jaeger and he spent the rest of the holiday there, returning home two days before the Elgars.

Rodewald attended the Three Choirs Festival of that year, which was held at Hereford. He stayed with Elgar and Schuster at the home of George R Sinclair, the organist at Hereford Cathedral.

On November 4 Elgar received a card from Rodewald, written quite cheerfully, saying that he thought he had influenza, but was over the fever and hoped to be well again soon. Three days later, however, a message arrived to say that Rodewald was unconscious and the doctors were not expecting him to recover. He was forty-three. On Monday the 9th Elgar travelled up to Liverpool. He did not go to Rodewald's house but went to see Adrian Mignot, President of the Liverpool Orchestral Society, who lived at No. 80 Huskisson Street.Mignot told him of Rodewald's death and Elgar, broken-hearted, walked the streets for hours. He found himself unable to return home and stayed at the North Western Hotel for the night. From here he wrote to Jaeger:

> Too late.
>   I stood it as long as I could & rushed up here — our dear, dear,

good friend passed away quietly at 12.30. I am heartbroken & cannot believe it. God bless him.

He was the dearest, kindest, *best* friend I ever had. I don't know how I write or what I've written — forgive me. I am utterly broken up.

Back once more at 'Craeg Lea' he wrote to Jaeger:

— yesterday I came home without seeing anyone & am now a wreck & broken-hearted man.

Do not send me any more score [ie, 'The Apostles'] — yet. I used to pass him every sheet as I finished it at Bettwys & heard his criticisms & altered passages to please him, God bless him!

... I can't say what I feel but I have lost my best & dearest — I thank heaven we all had that bit of time together in Wales you know a little of what he was.

Similar letters were written to Schuster and to Ernest Newman whom Elgar had met at Rodewald's house.

A few months later Elgar began to write some sketches of what was to become the slow movement of the *Second Symphony*. Alice heard in it a 'lament for dear Rodey and all human feeling'. Elgar had always intended to write an elegy for Rodewald and it was this majestic lament that served the purpose — a noble tribute to a great friend.

'Ridgehurst', Shenley, Hertfordshire

In 1901, at the Leeds Festival, Elgar made the acquaintance of Edward Speyer, a wealthy banker who had been born in Frankfurt but had become a naturalised British subject. In 1885 he married his second wife, Antonia Kufferath, a soprano singer and a great friend of Clara Schumann. He lived the life of a country gentleman, farming his 200 acres at his home at Shenley in Hertfordshire called 'Ridgehurst'. In his book *Edward Speyer. My Life and Friends* is the following description of the house where the Speyers moved on May 1 1893:

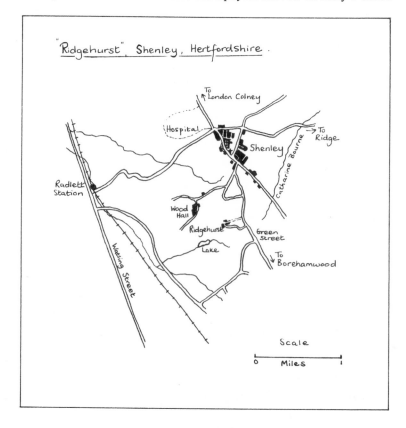

Early in 1893 we moved to a new home which I had purchased and which we were to inhabit for the next forty years. This was Ridgehurst, a place of some 200 acres, situated near the village of Shenley, in Hertfordshire, and some seventeen miles distant from London. The house, standing about 500 feet above sea-level, commanded an extensive view over a landscape of green pastures and woodlands unbroken by buildings of any kind, and an expanse of horizon ever changing in light and shade with clear and clouded skies. The attractions which this home offered to us were, on the one hand, the amenities of country life, an important factor considering our numerous family of young children, and, on the other, the easy distance from London. A much-prized feature of the house, itself of ample proportions, was an unusually large music room, originally a billiard room, of which ... we made good use.[1]

Elgar was to visit 'Ridgehurst' many times. It was for him not only a place of relaxation but also a place which stimulated him into creativity, as was 'The Hut'. The spacious house, built of pale-yellowish bricks, has a large, imposing porch supported by pillars. It stands in an impressive position and is approached by a long, narrow lane from the road near Green Street just out of Shenley village. Since Speyer's day it has been re-named and is now called 'Lyndhurst'. Soon after their first meeting Elgar dedicated a song, *Speak, Music*, written in 1901 with words by A C Benson, to 'Mrs. E. Speyer, Ridgehurst'.

Edward Speyer was a great help to his friend. In 1902, knowing that Elgar's music stood in the mainstream of European tradition, he arranged with the Duke of Meiningen that the Meiningen Orchestra, famous for its association with Wagner and Bayreuth, should bring their interpretation of the *Enigma Variations* under Fritz Steinbach to London. The Elgars were present at both concerts, which were given on October 17 and 18. Of Elgar, Steinbach was to say:

Here is an unexpected genius and pathfinder in the field of orchestration. Nowadays nearly every composer is content merely to adopt Wagner's innovations, but Elgar, as this work shows, is a real pioneer with a new technique in orchestration, combining entirely original effects with almost unique virtuosity.[2]

The following year, in January 1903, the Elgars were guests at 'Ridgehurst' and the Speyers were treated to excerpts from *The Apostles*, on which Elgar was hard at work. They were there from the

---

[1] pp 152−3.
[2] *Edward Speyer. My Life and Friends*, op cit, pp 174−5

Elgar rowing at 'Ridgehurst'.

13th until the 19th, but it was so cold that they were able to toboggan on the lake in the grounds. Elgar amused himself by playing duets with the pianist Leonard Borwick and played his piano piece *Skizze* to him.

Sir Edgar Speyer, a cousin of Edward, was also a patron of Elgar's. It was he who was instrumental in bringing Elgar into friendship with Richard Strauss. His home was at 46, Grosvenor Street, London, now the Japanese Embassy. Lady Speyer, his wife, was a professional violinist known as Leonora von Stosch. At Easter in 1910, when Elgar was working on the *Violin Concerto* at 'Ridgehurst', Lady Speyer played over the parts with him.

In May 1911, after returning from a trip to America, Elgar went to stay with the Speyers as he had to conduct some rehearsals with the London Symphony Orchestra. Laurence Binyon (whose words from his poem 'The Winnowing Fan' Elgar was to use in *The Spirit of England*) and Robert Hichens were there and Elgar enjoyed their congenial company and opposing them at billiards. Two months later he was at 'Ridgehurst' again, relaxing after his investiture at Buckingham Palace. This time the company consisted of P J Cobden-Sanderson — a 'most weird old gentleman & in weird clothes' — and Percy Grainger. In June 1912, Elgar continued his work on *The Music Makers* here as well as at 'The Hut'.

In the summer of 1919 Elgar spent a week at 'Ridgehurst', from July 8 – 15. Speyer's brother-in-law, Maurice Kufferath, manager of the Brussels Opera, was also staying there. Edward Speyer gives the following description of their time spent together:

> The two had never met before, but despite the bar of language they soon became fast friends, spending their days together from morning till night, doing music, fishing and walking.[1]

During the war years Sir Edgar Speyer had been attacked for allegedly having pro-German sympathies and was even accused of signalling to German submarines from his home in Norfolk. Elgar, however, backed him up, writing kindly to his friend in the midst of the outrage, for which the Speyers were most grateful.

However, after the war, and after Alice's death, Elgar found changes at 'Ridgehurst', as he had done at 'The Hut'. After a short visit in 1920 he wrote to Alice Stuart-Wortley:

> I cannot say that I appreciate the influx of *Germans* ... at Ridgehurst we had a German lady & her daughter who sang to the Germans in Brussels!!![2]

---

[1] *Edward Speyer. My Life and Friends*, op cit, p 223
[2] *Portrait of Elgar*, op cit, p 290

These were harsh words from one whose work had been championed by his German friends, but Elgar's whole outlook on life appeared to have become tinged with a certain bitterness. He now lived alone in a London flat and took to club life, seeing less of his old friends. Speyer, however, still wrote to him occasionally, although he was going blind. His failing eyesight and the bad weather prevented him from attending the luncheon held in Strauss's honour in 1922.

When Speyer was approaching 90 he invited Elgar and W H Reed down to 'Ridgehurst' for the weekend. Madame Guilhermina Suggia had also been invited to join them on the Saturday evening, Speyer presumably hoping for a musical weekend. Unfortunately, Elgar had just learnt a new type of billiard game, with which he was obsessed. After tea everyone had to go to the billiard table and learn the new game. During dinner the game was explained to Madame Suggia, who had just arrived, and consequently after coffee another game began involving her also. Reed continues the narrative thus:

> In vain poor Mr. Speyer produced some sheets of music to discuss with Sir Edward. They were glanced at hurriedly and put down again because it was his turn to play. The game went on until bedtime.
>
> The same thing happened next day. We played a new variation of the game for a while in the morning; then at last Mr. Speyer got in some interesting first-hand anecdotes about Brahms, Strauss, and others, which took us on until dinner. Mr. Speyer tried hard to get Edward into a musical mood. He even brought out some of his part-songs which he had there, hoping to interest him; but no: nothing could interest him for long except that new game, which we all played again until bedtime. Next morning, full of sincere thanks to our host and hostess for a most enjoyable week-end, and taking our farewell also of Madame Suggia, we left Elstree without having played a single note.[1]

In 1933, Elgar was at last to begin work on an opera, *The Spanish Lady*. As long ago as 1901 Speyer had asked Elgar about the prospect of writing an opera:

> How about the opera? Could the divine William not provide you with a libretto? It is true that 'Much ado about nothing' has been done already, but you may, I assume, find much ado about some other things![2]

Speyer had to wait until he was almost 94 to see his dream begun, Elgar choosing his libretto from Ben Jonson's *The Devil is an Ass*. By then, however, it was too late for the project ever to be fulfilled.

---

[1] *Elgar as I Knew Him*, op cit, p 52
[2] *Elgar O.M.*, op cit, p 238

'Ridgehurst' (front entrance).

'Ridgehurst' (back view).

Eventually 'Ridgehurst' became too large for comfort for the Speyers and they found it necessary to move. In his ninety-fifth year Speyer wrote at the end of his autobiography:

> Advancing age gradually rendered our life a quieter and more retired one. We left our large house and moved to Ridgehurst Lodge, a smaller one on the same estate. The pursuit of music, however, remained one of our chief interests, and was made possible by the frequent visits of many artist friends who still came and generously gave us of their best.[1]

He died on January 8 1934. Elgar was to outlive him by only a few weeks.

---

[1] *Edward Speyer. My Life and Friends,* op cit, p 232

Morecambe

In 1903, Elgar was approached to write a part-song as a test-piece for the Morecambe Festival and to adjudicate it. The Morecambe Festival had been born out of a music competition held as part of a church bazaar in 1891 and by the turn of the century had become one of the main musical festivals in the country. Elgar reluctantly consented and composed the part-song *Weary Wind of the West*, with words by T E Brown.

He disliked Morecambe when he arrived during the evening of April 30, but due to the great kindness of Canon Charles V Gorton, chairman of the festival, he was to enjoy his stay and was greatly surprised by the standards achieved. Canon Gorton was the son of the Archdeacon of Madras and became Rector of Morecambe in 1889. He was an indefatigable worker, renovating the church of St Laurence, daughter church to his own Holy Trinity and where the festivals were held; opening mission churches and each year preaching a festival sermon; originating the technical classes; and founding the Morecambe Art School. He entertained Elgar at his rectory opposite Holy Trinity and the two became firm and close friends.

The spacious, red-brick rectory, with its grey, tiled roof, was built in 1878. The date is carved in stone above the front doorway. It remains much as it did in Canon Gorton's day but a garage and rear kitchen were added on to the right wing in 1963. Elgar slept in the front bedroom on the left, which overlooks the sloping lawn at the side of the house, and had a dressing-room next door. His bedroom was above what was then the dining room, but is now the Rector's study.

The conductor of the Morecambe Musical Festival was R G H Howson, a local bank manager. He was also the principal administrator of the festival and was described by Elgar as 'the musical soul of the Morecambe affair'. Elgar's interest in the festival of 1903 gave him immense pleasure. Like Canon Gorton his enthusiasms were numerous. Gorton thought Morecambe should 'be made a place not only to trip to but to live in'[1] and he helped to establish the cricket club, golf clubs and the art and technical colleges, as well as directing the music at St Laurence's Church and conducting the Madrigal Society.

---

[1] Howson's obituary notice, June 30, 1905

The first performance of *Weary Wind of the West* was given on May 2. Elgar was delighted with the standard of the northern choirs who came to compete. In 1903, Hanley — singers whom Elgar knew well — won the chief competition by one point. *The Banner of St George* was also performed during the festival and the results were impressive:

> In rehearsing and performing his cantata Dr. Elgar did not find it necessary to make much allowance for the amateur status of the instrumentalists ... The behaviour of the enormous masses of competitors and listeners was in accord with the excellent record of former years.[1]

In all some 4,000 competitors took part and the sum total of audiences was around 6,000. Writing to Canon Gorton afterwards, on May 26, Elgar had this to say:

> DEAR CANON GORTON,
> I should like to thank you and the Committee for the very pleasant time I spent at the Morecambe Festival.
> I was delighted, & will add surprised, at the general excellence of the choral & orchestral work; the singing of the children especially was a revelation.
> In all the advanced classes there was displayed a quite uncommon appreciation of the poetical possibilities of the music, & the words were pronounced and (apparently) understood by the singers in a refreshingly sure way. Soon — a good day for art when it arrives — we shall all know the difference between sentiment & romance, and between what is theatrical & what is dramatic: these distinctions are unknown to many critics and to more performers — all of whom might have listened to a considerable portion of the Morecambe Festival with advantage.
> I cannot well express what I feel as to the immense influence your Festival must exert in spreading the love of music: it is rather a shock to find Brahms's part-songs appreciated & among the daily fare of a district apparently unknown to the sleepy London Press: people who talk of the spread of music in England & the increasing love of it rarely seem to know where the growth of the art is really strong and properly fostered. Some day the press will awake to the fact, already known abroad and to some few of us in England, that the living centre of music in Great Britain is not London, but somewhere farther North.
> ... In conclusion I will say it was a unique pleasure to hear so much that was truly admirable, & I look forward to the next Morecambe Festival with keen pleasure; I think it amply worth a long journey to be a listener, and as the enthusiasm is somewhat unusual to the eyes

---

[1] *The Musical Times*, June 1 1903

Composed for the Morecombe Musical Festival, May 1903

WEARY WIND OF THE WEST

Words by
T. E. BROWN*

Music by
EDWARD ELGAR

Morecambe Rectory.

---

of a chorally-starved southerner, may I say a spectator also?

I offer you a personal congratulation on the great organization you have called into being, & trust you may long be able to direct & advise your coadjutors.

      Believe me,
         Yours sincerely,
           EDWARD ELGAR.[1]

Elgar's criticism of the press may have been truthful, but it was rather a tactless way of putting things. Nevertheless, the letter shows most conclusively the obvious heights achieved by the musicians taking part.

Elgar was fortunate to meet Canon Gorton at this time, for he had been working hard on *The Apostles* since the beginning of the year. Canon Gorton subsequently read through the libretto and made several criticisms, to which Elgar later replied:

---

[1] Letter quoted in *The Musical Times*, July 1903, under the heading 'Somewhere Farther North'.

Of course *we* know the Resurrection was the climax, but I was trying to look at it from the point of view of the weak man of the time ... I have endeavoured to suggest that forgiveness is for *all who repent*. To my mind *Judas'* crime and sin was *despair* (Ibsen etc. etc.); not only the betrayal which was done for a worldly purpose.[1]

Canon Gorton's aid, however, was much appreciated by Elgar. From August 3–5 1903 he visited Malvern to discuss further theological points. Elgar wrote of him to Jaeger the day he left: 'he is a fine man so jolly & clever'.

Elgar travelled to Morecambe in 1904 on April 28 and stayed until May 2. Frank Schuster also attended the festival; they stayed at the Grand Hotel. On April 30, Elgar's *Five Part-Songs from the Greek Anthology* were performed, only five days after their first performance, at the Royal Albert Hall.

In 1905 Elgar thought it was going to be impossible for him to attend the Morecambe Festival, but in the end he arranged the visit so as not to disappoint his northern friends. This time Alice accompanied him and they were there from May 17–22. Although they appear to have stayed in a hotel they spent a good deal of time with the Gortons. The first night they attended a concert in the evening and the following day lunched at the rectory. On the 19th Alice again lunched with the the Gortons but Elgar, busy rehearsing for *King Olaf*, ate at the Midland Hotel. There seem to have been some problems with the orchestra for this concert, but after the performance Alice wrote in her diary: 'Splendid chorus in evening & J. Coates magnificent. Orch rather better'. Afterwards they had supper with Canon Gorton. They lunched at the rectory again the next day before Elgar presented the Challenge Shield and made a speech and Alice gave away the prizes. On the Sunday (May 21) Elgar went for a walk with Canon Gorton and they visited Mr Howson, who had only a few weeks to live, before having supper again at the rectory. They left at 12.30 pm the next day and had to suffer a long, cold journey home.

In October of that year Elgar was asked to become Mayor of Hereford. He consulted Canon Gorton about his decision. His acceptance would have incurred difficulties as Elgar was a Catholic, but in any case Canon Gorton was against the plan for the reason that he thought it would interfere with Elgar's 'gift for prophecy — in music'. Elgar therefore declined the honour.

For the Morecambe Festival of 1906, Elgar composed a part-song entitled *Evening Scene* with words by Coventry Patmore. He had in

---

[1] *The Musical Times*, October 1903

fact completed it by the end of August 1905. On August 24 of that year he wrote to Jaeger:

> You will receive ... a new part-song — my best bit of landscape so far in that line. You won't make anything of it on the P.F. — Morecambe is the place to hear it.

In reply Jaeger said he found it 'a perfect gem of a picture', reminding him of Schubert's *Der Leiermann*. The song was dedicated to the memory of Howson, who died in June 1905, and it was given its first performance at the festival on May 12 1906. Elgar was unable to be present as he was in America. Later that year Canon Gorton visited the Three Choirs Festival at Hereford.

On January 1 1907 the Elgars travelled to Capri with Canon Gorton, who was acting British chaplain at the time, before continuing their journey to Rome. Here, in February, Elgar composed a part-song entitled *There is sweet music*, with words by Tennyson from *The Lotus Eaters*. He dedicated it to Canon Gorton and it was published by Novello in the following year.

Alice accompanied Elgar to Morecambe again for the Festival of 1907. They arrived on May 1 at about 5 o'clock but Alice found it a 'dreary place'. They were entertained for lunch at the rectory and on the 3rd Elgar paid a visit to Lancaster. On May 6 they returned home. This was to be their last visit.

Canon Gorton retired in 1908 when his health broke down, and Elgar and George Sinclair found a house for him and his family in Hereford early in 1909. He died tragically on August 20 1912 when the partial and painful type of paralysis from which he was suffering caused him to stumble as he tried to rise from his wheelchair, in which he had been placed overlooking the River Wye. He fell into the river and, despite his son Neville's brave attempts to rescue him, was drowned.

PART II

HOLIDAYS IN GREAT BRITAIN

Isle of Wight

After their wedding at the London Oratory on May 8 1889, Alice and Edward travelled to the Isle of Wight for a three-week honeymoon. They stayed first at Shanklin and then moved to Ventnor, one of the fashionable resorts of the day, where they stayed at 3, Alexandra Gardens. The bay-windowed guest house occupies a superb elevated position in a private road overlooking the sea. Miss Horsford, daughter of the landlady of the time, wrote to Carice on the death of Elgar:

> Sir Edward and your mother had the drawing-room floor & won all our praise for their simplicity and lack of ostentation or 'swank'. I remember they left a very appreciative & flattering account of their visit to us which I would give a good deal to have preserved ... The recollection of your father's visit will be green in my memory until my own call comes.[1]

In Ventnor, Elgar bought his wife a copy of Moritz's *Travels in England in 1782*. On May 14 he wrote in his diary: '*Had to wade. Kissed her wet foot*'. (Alice was to remember this incident the week she died.) The following Saturday, May 18, the *Isle of Wight Advertiser* published a 'Fashionable List of Visitors and Residents for Ventnor & Its Environs corrected up to May 16th'. An entry for number 3, Alexandra Gardens, read: *Mr. and Mrs. Edward Elgar, Kensington, marked with an asterisk to denote that they were fresh

---

[1] *Alice Elgar, Enigma of a Victorian Lady*, Percy Young, p 101

arrivals. Naturally the Elgars bought a copy and sent it off to Worcester. Elgar wrote a letter from Ventnor to his friend Dr Charles Buck:

> This is a time of deep peace & happiness to me after the vain imaginings of so many years & the pessimistic views so often unfolded to you on the Settle highways have vanished! God wot![1]

They returned to London at the end of the month and moved into rented rooms at 3, Marloes Road, Kensington.

In 1980 a commemorative plaque was erected on the house at 3, Alexandra Gardens (now called the Bermuda Guest House) by the present proprietors. It reads:

Sir
Edward Elgar
Composer
Stayed here
in 1889

---

[1] *Letters of Edward Elgar and other writings*, ed Percy Young, p43

'The White Lion', Patterdale.

Lake District

Elgar spent many holidays in the 1880s with Dr Charles Buck at his home in North Yorkshire. They would often visit the Lake District and stay at 'The White Lion' in Patterdale. The beautiful scenery inspired Elgar into creativity and in 1885 he began to write a 'Lakes' overture as a result of his visit to Lake Windermere. In July 1912, in the *Yorkshire Weekly Post*, Dr Buck recalled the effect that the visit had on Elgar:

> Not a word could be got out of him, and then suddenly he began to write furiously. When he had finished he said that he had never known quite the same sensation before, and that he was simply obliged to write.

Unfortunately this manuscript has been lost.

* * *

The Lake District was to remain a favourite haunt of Elgar after his marriage. On August 24 1911, Elgar travelled alone to Penrith, and on the following days paid visits to Ullswater and Grasmere. Alice joined him on the 28th and they stayed at the 'Lake Hotel' in Keswick. Three days later they visited Patterdale, when Elgar was able to show Alice 'The White Lion', where he had spent such happy times years before. They returned home on September 2.

* * *

The following year they spent another short holiday in the Lakes after the Birmingham Festival, arriving at Grasmere on October 5. They stayed at the 'Prince of Wales Lake Hotel' with its beautiful position overlooking Rydal Water. Here they enjoyed themselves rowing and walking, Alice especially delighting in a walk to Loughrig Tarn.

On September 6 1915, Elgar travelled via Penrith again to Grasmere and Ullswater for four days. He then drove from Grasmere to Coniston and caught the train to Millom in order to get to Ravenglass, where he met his wife, and Alice Stuart-Wortley, who was on holiday there. From here in the next few days they visited Wast Water, Furness Abbey and Calder Abbey and Seascale further up the coast, which Alice thought a 'horrid little place'. In a letter to Walford Davies, Elgar said that they were 'trying to find a little rest and peace'. The Elgars then returned to Grasmere for a further three days before they left the area, Elgar going on to Hereford and Alice returning to 'Severn House'.

* * *

In the August of 1916, again to escape the ravages of war in London, they returned to Ullswater. On the 11th they met Lalla Vandervelde (Edward Speyer's daughter), who stayed with them for the next few days. In her diary Alice describes the following incident, which took place after they had seen Lalla off:

> Very nice on the lake. A storm came on & E and A sat at the end of bench on boat very close together & very happy under one umbrella, & a man who had been standing by talking to another suddenly said, putting his face close to theirs, 'You are lᴜvers still like me and my wife'. A. rather speechless with surprise. E. said in a sweet way 'I hope so'. It was quite sincere & very touching.

They returned home on August 21, probably little realising that this would be their last visit together to this favourite corner of England.

The Southern Counties

Sussex

At the end of April 1894 the Elgars left Worcestershire for a holiday in Sussex. They visited Littlehampton, Chichester, Brighton and Arundel, returning to Arundel later to stay for two days at the Arundel Hotel. They were impressed with the town, dominated by its castle, and saw the keep. On the same day, after lunching at the Norfolk Arms, they visited the Roman Catholic Cathedral Church of S Philip Neri. Huge in dimension, it was built by the Norfolk family during 1869–73 in French Gothic style. The Elgars also enjoyed walking in the thousand-acre park. Edward went to the golf links a great deal to enjoy one of his favourite sports.

Later in life the Elgars were to become much more familiar with the area when they rented a cottage in Sussex in May 1917 called 'Brinkwells'. Here, in remote woods near the village of Fittleworth, Elgar was in his element. As Dr Percy Young has written in his book *Elgar O.M.*:

> ... Elgar went to Sussex to avoid people rather than to meet them. The countryside was his great joy — and inspiration. He loved the setting and the ancient buildings of the downland villages — Petworth, Pulborough, Storrington, Findon and Amberley; the larger monuments of Arundel and Chichester; the remains of antiquity that were to be seen near Stane Street. Most of all he loved the water — of streams and lakes in which he could fish — and the woods.[1]

Dorset

At the beginning of May 1897, Alice and Elgar went for a week's holiday in Dorset, when they visited Bournemouth and Christchurch and spent a few days at Poole harbour. Elgar enjoyed himself playing a good deal of golf again, and they both spent many happy hours walking and relaxing.

Hampshire

On August 15 1912, Mrs Winifred Murray, a friend of Alice and

---

[1] p191

Carice's, came to lunch at 'Severn House' and afterwards drove the Elgars to her home in Hampshire. It was a beautiful day and they had a glorious drive, especially over Hindhead, to Mrs Murray's home at Steep. The village stands on top of a hill where a group of yews, one at least 600 years old, stand guard by the little church which dates from Norman times. Elgar loved it and was charmed by Mrs Murray's house, 'Little Langleys', with its attractive garden.

The following day they drove to Chithurst on the River Rother, Alice especially enjoying the pine trees and the glorious heather. On the 17th Mrs Murray drove them over the South Downs to Southsea, where they walked along the sea front and after tea visited the castle. Alice was reminded of the times she had spent here with her mother and cousins. For the next couple of days, Elgar worked hard at 'Little Langleys' orchestrating *The Music Makers*, which he finished on the 21st. The next day they left regretfully for home, again enjoying wonderful views from Hindhead. When they arrived back in London, Elgar took Alice and Mrs Murray to lunch at the Pall Mall Restaurant and then the ladies went off to the London Library whilst Elgar went to Novellos to discuss the new work.

Isle of Man

In the spring of 1914, Elgar went with his wife to spend a week in the Isle of Man. Elgar, along with Granville Bantock, had been invited to adjudicate the music festival held there. On Sunday March 29 they left London for Liverpool, and the following day sailed across to Douglas on what Alice described as a 'horrid little steamer'. They were entertained by Lord Raglan at Government House.

Elgar was called upon to adjudicate on April 1. Alice's entry in her diary for that date reads: 'E adjudicated very well & said nice things to the people. Gran. Bantock did same'. The next day they went to the Opera House as Elgar had to rehearse for a performance of his cantata *The Banner of St George*. Apparently the chorus were fine but they found the orchestra 'extraordinary'.

On April 3 they were shown around the historical sites of the island by Lord Raglan, who drove them to Castletown, Peel and Tynwald. They returned home the following day. This was the only visit they paid to the Isle of Man.

Scotland

Elgar first went to Scotland in 1883 at the age of 26 when he visited Inverness and obviously spent some time there with a woman he met. His composition *Une Idylle* (op 4. No 1.), written that year and published in 1885, is dedicated to 'Miss E.E., Inverness'. When questioned later about this lady by Dr Charles Buck, Elgar replied:

> Now as to your queries as aforesaid — Miss E. E. of Inverness is nobody — that is to say that I shall ever see again. I wrote down the little air when I was there & dedicated it to her 'with estimation the most profound' as a Frenchman would say, that's all.[1]

However, he did return to Scotland in 1884, when he travelled to Glasgow, Rothesay, Oban, Inverness, Stirling and Edinburgh and also spent some time visiting the islands of Staffa and Iona. Whether or not he saw Miss E. E. again in Inverness is unknown. He had nevertheless been very despondent and wanted to think out his future on this visit. He decided that a career as a solo violinist was not for him and resolved to resign his position as bandmaster at the County Lunatic Asylum at Powick and devote more time to composition. Thus in 1885 he wrote a *Scottish Overture* which he hoped to get performed at one of Stockley's Birmingham concerts, but he failed to convince the conductor of its worth. Writing to Buck again he says:

> Oh! about the Scotch overture — I have turned it up. I don't know if I told you about it before — I showed it to old Stockley & he candidly said he could not read the Score & it sounded to him disconnected. So I have retired into my shell & live in hopes of writing a polka someday — failing that a single chant is probably my fate.[2]

The manuscript has been lost.

* * *

In July 1914 the Elgars went to Scotland with their daughter for a family holiday, as Elgar had been unwell. They left London on the 19th, travelling overnight to Glasgow and then went on to Inverness. They had booked for two weeks at Lairg, but on their arrival did not like the place or the hotel, so they took another train to Achnasheen and then took a taxi for the 30-mile drive to Gairloch in Ross-shire. This turned out to be rather a nerve-shattering experience for Elgar and Carice as the driver was slightly drunk and kept driving very near

---

[1] Letter dated March 8 1885
[2] Letter dated January 8 1886

the edges of deep precipices. Alice, however, sat in the front seat quite unperturbed! They arrived eventually at the Gairloch Hotel, which has a perfect setting at the foot of craggy cliffs and overlooks the sea across Gairloch Bay to the Isle of Skye. They all adored the place. Elgar wrote to Alice Stuart-Wortley: 'The wild birds feed their young within 30 yards of this window – gannets, oyster catchers and divers and a dozen others.' Alice was also enchanted and wrote to Troyte Griffith:

> This is the most wonderfully beautiful place we have ever been in except Bavaria. We look straight across to Skye, an ever varying object, sometimes shimmering grey, sometimes magically blue, & the mountain views are gorgeous. I wish you were here to walk & talk & sketch. Edward & C. are out in a boat on the sea, fishing. I went with them yesterday afternoon but found it rather monotonous for 3 hours at a time. This morning they were enlivened by a sudden visit of those dear porpoises jumping & snorting quite close. This place is so mercifully untouched. There is only a scrambly bank down to the beach, no made path even, & the gulls fish and bathe & sleep close by, from our window E. watched a stork-like bird fish & swallow fish surround[ed] by an eager crowd of small gulls at 3 a.m. & the sheep wander down & lie on the sand at the water's edge & this morning early a rabbit was quietly sitting out close by.
>
> I hope we shall be able to stay some little time & there cd. hardly be a more inspiring place for E. & he loves it. He cannot stay in one minute![1]

Elgar spent some time considering an offer by Henry Embleton, a wealthy supporter of the Leeds Choral Union, for the third part of the oratorio trilogy as a commission for his choir. The outbreak of war on August 4 put an end to any plans he may have had. Elgar had telegraphed for information to Alice Stuart-Wortley about the rumours that were reaching them. On the 6th he wrote to her:

> The spirit of the men is splendid, the Seaforths went first, later in the week the mounted Lovats Scouts rode through — were given a sort of meal here by the manageress & rode off in the moonlight by the side of the loch & disappeared into the mountains ... I *wish* I could go to the front but they may find some menial occupation for a worthless person.

They wanted to return home immediately but had to wait several days for a car to take them the 30 miles back to the railway station. On their journey back to London they were able to watch the troop-trains passing through Inverness and Edinburgh. Elgar returned to find that *Land of Hope and Glory* had become a second national anthem.

---

[1] Letter dated July 29 1914

Gairloch Hotel, Ross-shire.

Wales

In August 1901, Rosa Burley, headmistress of 'The Mount' school in Malvern, where Elgar taught the violin, took a house at Llangranog, a remote seaside village in Cardiganshire (now Dyfed). She invited Elgar to spend some time with her family there and Elgar, having been rather depressed of late, accepted the invitation. Llangranog is situated in the small valley of the tiny River Hawen. The stone cottages are arranged on either side of the road which follows the narrow valley down to the sea. The nature of this valley means that it has been almost impossible for the village to expand, and therefore it must look much the same today as when Elgar visited it 80 years ago.

Rosa Burley left two accounts of this holiday, the first published in *Letters to Nimrod* in 1965 and the second in *Edward Elgar: the record of a friendship*, written in 1948 and published in 1972. There are some discrepancies between these two accounts. According to the biography, Elgar left for Llangranog on Thursday August 15, travelling from Great Malvern to Henllan, the nearest station, 14 miles from Llangranog. He left on the 8.09 am, which was the first train out of Great Malvern, and had to change at Hereford, Newport and Carmarthen, where he had to wait two hours for the train at 5.20 pm to Henllan, arriving at 6.29 pm. The final part of the journey was completed in a farmer's cart which had been sent to meet him. According to the account in *Letters to Nimrod*, on arrival at the village Elgar was too nervous to drive down the steep hill-road which dropped down to the bay, so he got out and walked. By the time he arrived he was in the highest spirits. Lady Elgar's diary records that he arrived sometime after ten. If this account of the journey is correct it raises some doubt about the authenticity of Rosa Burley's account, published in *Letters to Nimrod*, of Elgar's arrival at Carmarthen station when he demanded a ticket to 'a little station halfway up the line'. When told that no train stopped there, Elgar produced a timetable to show that on Wednesdays and Thursdays the 1.15 train stopped by request. Accordingly he left on this train and at Henllan the station-master and the porter came out to meet it. The sight of them reminded the engine driver that he should have stopped and he had to reverse the engine back into the station in order to allow Elgar to alight. This story is not verified by the Great Western timetable for July–September 1901. There was no train out of Carmarthen at 1.15 and all trains on the line were given stopping times at Henllan. He should not have had to buy another ticket at Carmarthen as Henllan was a

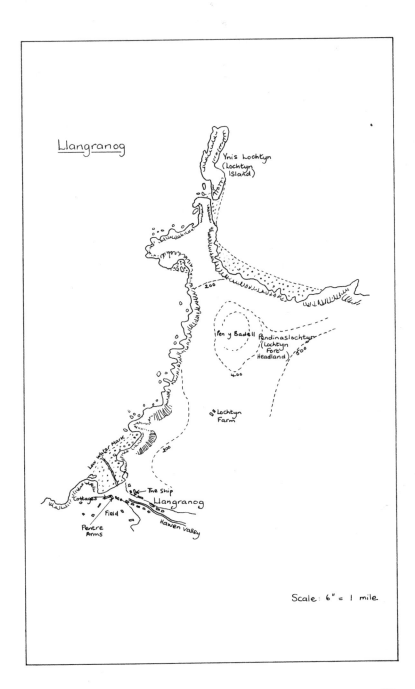

Llangranog

Ynis Lochtyn
(Lochtyn
Island)

200

Pen y Badell   Pendinaslochtyn
(Lochtyn
Fort
Headland)

400   500

Lochtyn
Farm

Low Water Mark

200

Cottages   The Ship
            Llangranog
    Field
Pentre   Hawen valley
Arms

Scale: 6" = 1 mile.

83

station on the Great Western, as was Great Malvern. It is most likely that this account was added to much later by Rosa Burley, probably with a certain amount of romanticism, for in this account she refers to him as 'Sir Edward' whilst elsewhere he is merely called 'Edward'.

It was impossible to put Elgar up in the same house as Miss Burley had taken, as it was also occupied by her mother and sister, some South African nephews and nieces and a pupil. She therefore invited him to stay in a neighbouring cottage and to eat with them at meal times. The house stood on the edge of the shore, next door to the inn, which was probably the 'Pentre Arms'. The pub is still there and used to have a house next door which was rented for summer visitors. The house itself is now part of the pub. It is possible that Elgar stayed in one of the row of four cottages next to the 'Pentre Arms' (the first one being occupied by Miss Burley's party) as there are no other cottages nearby. However, although in the biography she says that rooms were available in a neighbouring cottage, in *Letters to Nimrod* she speaks of a 'bedroom in the village'. North of the village is a peninsula called Pendinaslochtyn ('Lochtyn fort headland') and at the end of this is a small island, Ynis Lochtyn. According to Rosa Burley the house had a view across the bay to this island, which was only visible at low tide, when Elgar and the others often waded out to it. Ynis Lochtyn is, however, definitely not visible from the bay, is difficult to reach at low tide and would be hazardous to climb.

Elgar was really delighted with the place — which in a letter to Jaeger he called 'Llangringoggywoggypygwgssill',[1] enjoying the sea and scenery, the Welsh mutton, the local vegetables bought from the villagers, the mushrooms growing in plenty in the valleys and the easily accessible shellfish:

> We rigged up a bathing suit for him out of an old pair of pyjamas and he did not mind when my little neice told him that he looked like a monkey!
> We were in and out of the water all day. The children went off in the boats after lobster pots, and the often got shrimps in the bay. There were mussels and winkles on the rocks. Edward was quite unrecognisable — he shouted with glee and played about like a little boy.[2]

The men of the village would gather by the sea-wall in the evening, often breaking into a hymn in four-part harmony. One day, whilst out walking on the seashore, the sound of distant singing reached them from a group of people on a hillside across the bay. No melodic line

---

[1] Letter dated Wednesday August 14 1901
[2] *Letters to Nimrod*, ed Percy Young, p 142

Llangranog village — looking south-west.

could be identified at that distance, but there was the frequent drop of a third which Elgar thought typical of Welsh music. This idea was to remain with him and he appeared to have a Welsh Overture in mind, indicated by the suggested scoring of the 'Welsh' melody in his sketch-book, which is also inscribed Ynis Llochtryn' (sic). Later, however, the idea was to be used as the second subject in his *Introduction and Allegro for String Orchestra*.

The first performance of the *Introduction and Allegro* was given in the Queen's Hall on March 8 1905. Elgar wrote the performance notes himself:

Some three years ago, in Cardiganshire, I thought of writing a brilliant piece for string orchestra. On the cliff, between blue sea and blue sky, thinking out my theme, there came up to me the sound of singing. The songs were too far away to reach me distinctly, but one point common to all was impressed upon me, and led me to think, perhaps wrongly, that it was a real Welsh idiom — I mean the fall of a third —

Fitting the need of the moment I made the tune which appears in the Introduction and in the coda of this work; and so my gaudery became touched with romance. The tune may therefore be called, as is the melody in the overture 'In the South', a *canto popolare*, but the suggesting country in this case is Wales, and not Italy.

The sketch was forgotten until a short time ago, when it was brought to my mind by hearing, far down our own Valley of the Wye, a song similar to those so pleasantly heard on Ynis Lochtyn. The singer of the Wye unknowingly reminded me of my sketch. This I have now completed and, although there may be (and I hope there is) a Welsh feeling in the one theme — to quote Shakespeare again: — 'All the waters in the Wye cannot wash the Welsh blood out of its body'[1] — the work is really a tribute to 'that sweet borderland where I have made my home'.

Although Elgar describes that he heard the singing on Ynis Lochtyn, it is possible that he mistook the name of the island for the name of the whole area north of the village, which is known as Lochtyn or Lochdyn, so that he is in fact referring to the cliff leading up to the old fort. In the *Letters to Nimrod* account Rosa Burley says: 'as we looked across the bay we saw a party of folk on the hillside ... presently we heard them singing.' Elgar's own description of being 'on the cliff, between blue sea and blue sky' and of the sound of singing coming 'up' to him points further to the fact that they must have been on the mainland as Ynis Lochtyn is below the level of the main peninsula. A field on the opposite side of the bay was often used for practice by singers and it is therefore possible that this was where Elgar heard the singing.

Elgar left Llangranog on Monday August 19, presumably travelling with Miss Burley and her party, as Lady Elgar records in her diary that Elgar 'spent night at the Mount'. The following day he went to 'Birchwood Lodge'. Alice writes on August 20 — 'E. arrived all safely D.G. about 12.30.'

* * *

After Elgar had returned from his trip to America at the end of May 1906, and had just sustained the death of his father, the doctor ordered that he have a complete change and insisted on a holiday. Alice decided on New Radnor. They went on June 12, but on the 25th Elgar slipped on some wet stones and hurt his shoulder. This shook him a great deal and he told Littleton, his publisher, that he was too overdone to finish *The Kingdom*. He was sent home to bed but then fortunately recovered fairly quickly.

---

[1] *Henry V*, Act IV, sc vii

* * *

On December 5 1906 the Elgars went on a 'very rough, stormy day' to Llandrinod Wells so that Elgar could take the waters. At the turn of the century it was fashionable for English society to visit Llandrinod Wells, where it was hoped the legendary mineral waters would relieve a host of ailments. The town boasted crescents of large elegant houses, spacious hotels and wide roads, but Alice, arriving on a bad day after a terrible journey, decided the town was ugly and uninteresting, although she admitted there were fine distant views. The shops were shut and there were no cabs, so she had to go out in the rain to find a hotel. They disliked the hotel she chose and thought of returning home the following day, but then they went to see the 'Gwalia Hotel' and decided to stay there.

Elgar drank the waters, hoping for a cure from his ills. He wrote to Sidney Colvin:

> We met like ghouls in the pump-room at 7.30 am in the dark: mysterious and strange; hooded and cloaked we quaffed smoking brine and sulphur and walked thro' dim-lit woods, some-times in snow.[1]

Alice returned home on the 10th but Elgar remained another five days; however, they spoke to each other on the telephone every day.

Elgar was to make several visits here, but returning after his trip to Italy in March 1913 he decided the waters were not doing him good.

* * *

On August 12 1907, Elgar, Alice and Carice left for a ten-day holiday in Wales. The next day they arrived in Barmouth and took some rooms, but it was so misty and windy that they nearly returned home. They tried to get rooms on the 15th in Tywyn, further down the coast, which they thought a lovely place, but failed to find any, so the next day they went north to Harlech. Elgar decided they would return home if they couldn't find any rooms there, but in the end they were successful and stayed until the 22nd. During the train journey home Elgar and Carice played together in the corridor. Alice's diary records: 'E. fell full length. A. laughed so much sh. cd. not even urge him to rise before someone came down the corridor'.

* * *

---

[1] *Edward Elgar: His Life and Music*, Diana M McVeagh, p46

From August 5 to September 1 1913 the Elgars went to North Wales to imbibe the sea air and to give Elgar a change. They chose to stay at Penmaen-mawr, but had rather a dismal holiday. The house where they stayed was called 'Tan-yr-allt' (Under the Hill), but it was damp and miserable and there was a continual north-west wind. However, they made trips to Conway, Caernarvon and Anglesey, which they enjoyed. Elgar spent a good deal of the time revising his notes and correcting the proofs of *Falstaff*, which was to be performed at Leeds on October 2. They were glad to return home, however, although sorry to leave the sea. Alice wrote on September 1: 'Very glad to leave the house which we disliked. Very much delighted to leave the disagreeable Welsh'. The day after their return Elgar wrote to Troyte Griffith:

> We arrived home last night glad enough to shake the mud off us — the mud of Wales I mean.

This was to be the last family holiday in Wales.

PART III
HOLIDAYS ABROAD

France

Elgar's first visit abroad was to Paris in the summer of 1880, where he went with Charles Pipe, who was to become his brother-in-law in the following year. They heard Saint-Saëns play the organ at La Madeleine and also saw the play *Malade Imaginaire* by Molière. It appears that he met a woman here, for he recalled the romance many years later after visiting Paris in 1933:

> I decided to go to the Barbizon, but when I passed the cross-roads the longing had passed away. That belonged to the romance of 1880, now dead.[1]

This visit to France was to inspire him to write a set of five quadrilles entitled *Paris*, which were dedicated to Miss Holloway, the organist of the Powick hospital where Elgar was bandmaster. The titles of the quadrilles are: 1) *Chatelet* 2) *L'Hippodrome* 3) *Alcazar d'Eté (Champs Elysées)* 4) *La! Suzanne!* 5) *Café des Ambassadeurs: La femme de l'emballeur.*

* * *

Elgar, his wife and daughter went to Italy for a holiday in the April of 1909, but Elgar went on ahead on April 9 to spend a few days on his own at the 'Hotel des deux Mondes' in Paris. Alice and Carice travelled over on the 17th and the next day they went to High Mass at La Madeleine. Elgar wrote from here to Canon Gorton on April 19:

> Paris is alive &, in a curious way, inspiring: all cities are built on seven something. Rome on seven hills, Hereford (!) on the cardinal virtues I suppose very much buried & Paris certainly on the seven deadly sins — which make life worth *looking* at if not worth living.

---

[1] *The Daily Telegraph*, July 1 1933

The following day they left the hotel and continued on their journey to Florence.[1]

* * *

In May 1924, Elgar went to Paris with Henry Embleton, the Leeds Choir and the London Symphony Orchestra to conduct *The Dream of Gerontius*, the *Second Symphony* and *Sea Pictures*. Two concerts were given in Paris and one on the way back, at the Casino in Dieppe. The crossing from Newhaven to Dieppe was very choppy. Elgar was quite unaffected by the voyage and insisted on giving his cabin to W H Reed, who was rather overcome, looking after him all through the four-hour trip. The hotel where Elgar stayed was near the tomb of the Unknown Warrior and the Leeds Choir laid a huge wreath, intertwined with the French and English colours, on the tomb. W H Reed, in his book *Elgar as I Knew Him*, recalls the incident of an American lady staying in the hotel asking about the wreath. He explained the reason for their visit and persuaded her to buy tickets for the concert in the afternoon when Elgar was to conduct his *Second Symphony*. The concert was very well attended; Elgar received a great ovation and returned feeling very hot in a taxi to the hotel. Immediately the American lady accosted him and told him how 'too thrilled' she had been and how 'too cute' the Scherzo was, etc. Without answering Elgar stared at her and went upstairs to his room. Reed was left to explain to the lady how wrought-up Elgar was after a concert and promised to bring him back down after he had changed and introduce her to him properly. After pleading unsuccessfully with Elgar for a while, Reed continues:

> With all the pathos I could summon up, I demanded, 'Is she to go back to America with a completely wrong impression of you — you of all people! — who I know would never hurt anyone's feelings wilfully?' That moved him to reply, 'Where is she now?' he said. 'We will go and speak to her'. I formally introduced her to him; he spoke to her in his most charming manner without referring to his previous behaviour; and she, let us hope, felt consoled, and perhaps honoured by the experience.[2]

* * *

---

[1] See p 125   [2] p 77

Elgar about to fly to Paris, 1933.

In 1933, Elgar travelled to Paris by aeroplane with Richard Mountford, his valet, and Fred Gaisberg of the Gramophone Company. It was his first flight and he thoroughly enjoyed it, spending the two-and-a-quarter hours in the air from Croydon to Le Bourget, completing a crossword puzzle. He went in order to conduct a performance of the *Violin Concerto* with the young Yehudi Menuhin on May 31 at the Salle Pleyel. It was to be a great occasion. The Diplomatic Corps had been invited to attend and Yehudi's father wrote to Fred Gaisberg:

I am happy to tell you that ex-premier Herriot (who expects to be the premier again by May 31st and who at any rate is the power behind the throne' now) has arranged already for the President, Premier, etc., to attend the May 31st concert. Thus the beginning of the Gala affair is reassured, as it will be THE social event of the Spring season, and the full house being Yehudi's always in Paris, we have every reason to believe that our dear Sir Edward Elgar will draw a lot of joy and contentment of this visit with us. Do please convey to him in your own way this message, as you will know how to break it nicely without at the same time making it appear that we pray about it.

For after all, things should come that way on the score of sheer merit of the dear, lovely, fine soul that Sir Edward is.[1]

Elgar was entertained by the Menuhins and one of Yehudi's dearest recollections of his visit was the breakfasts they shared together at his home in Ville d'Avray on the outskirts of Paris. Yehudi played magnificently and Elgar was thrilled by his performance.

Elgar also paid a visit to Delius at his home at Grez-sur-Loing, partly out of sympathy and partly because his interest in the parts of Yorkshire both he and Delius knew had recently been revived by letters from Dr Charles Buck. He took Delius records of music by Sibelius and Wolf as a present. Writing later that year to Norman O'Neill, Elgar said of his visit:

I was delighted to see Delius in his home & am glad he allowed me the privilege, although it involved 80 miles in a French taxi; the prospect of seeing him made the journey a light matter.[2]

Eric Fenby has left the following account of their meeting in his book *Delius as I knew him*:

Elgar came. It was really delightful. He stayed from tea-time until nearly seven o'clock. He was very genial and natural and altogether quite unlike what I had expected him to be. I never knew him well. ... We talked about music. I told Elgar that I had just finished the Idyll with your help, and he was very interested in the way we managed to work and asked a great deal about you. He said he was sorry that he'd missed you. He then went on to say that he was busy working on his Third Symphony.

'But then,' he added, 'my music will not interest you, Delius; you are too much of a poet for a workman like me!'

... We talked about books (and I could see that he was very well read), about people we'd known, about what would grow in my garden

[1] *Elgar O.M.*, op cit, pp 226–7
[2] Letter dated December 22 1933

Elgar with Georges Enesco and Yehudi Menuhin.

Elgar with the Menuhin family and friends.

and what would not grow in his in England. He was as excited as a schoolboy about his first trip from Croydon to Paris by air and insisted that, should I go to England again, I must travel by air. He would love to conduct some of my music. Would I send him some scores? I said that I would and that it would give me the greatest of pleasure. We had a bottle of champagne before he left, and I was very disappointed that he couldn't stay longer, but he had to motor back to Paris to see young Yehudi Menuhin that night.

'The way that boy plays my concerto is amazing,' said Elgar. Obviously I could see that he adored the youngster. Most of the time he sat close by me on a very modest chair, the one my man generally uses, and, as Jelka afterwards told me, he constantly telegraphed signs to her — was he tiring me? — was he to leave? — but, of course, she negatived them. Yes, I liked Elgar very much ...'[1]

In *The Daily Telegraph* Elgar wrote of Delius:

To me he seemed like the poet who, seeing the sun again after his pilgrimage, had found complete harmony between will and desire.[2]

Both Elgar and Delius were to have only one more year to live.

---

[1] pp 123–5
[2] July 1 1933

Delius's home at Grez-sur-Loing, near Paris.

Germany

Elgar travelled to Leipzig for a fortnight's holiday, arriving just before midnight in the last few minutes of 1882. Entering the Hotel Sedan with his overcoat, travelling-cap and umbrella, a waiter mistook him for a New Year guest at a private party. He was shown into the private room where at that moment the people were standing on chairs shouting 'Prosit Neujahr'. Elgar bowed nervously, turned round and departed as quickly as possible!

Apparently he had an 'adventurous journey', according to a letter to Dr Charles Buck. Later in the same letter he writes:

> I heard no end of stuff. Schumann principally & Wagner no end. They have a good opera in Leipzig & we went many times.[1]

The 'we' refers to the fact that he was accompanied by Helen Weaver, daughter of the proprietor of a shoe shop at 84, High Street, Worcester, who was studying at the Leipzig Conservatory of Music and whom he referred to as his 'Braut' — and also by a seventeen-year-old English girl, who was to become Mrs Edith Wood-Somers of 'Applethorpe', Blewbury, Berkshire. His chief reason for visiting Leipzig was to see Helen, and his friendship with her lasted until 1885. Elgar always referred to Edith as 'The Infant'. One evening they decided to visit the opera to hear Anton Rubinstein conducting one of his own works. Edith offered to get the tickets, which she did, and then Elgar asked her what time they should eat. In a letter to Carice many years later, Edith recalled the incident, replying as follows:

> 'Oh, before six, as we must be at the theatre at 6.30'. I remember how very astonished he looked, but we duly had supper at 5.45 and were on the doorstep at 6.15. I was greatly excited about it all (only seventeen), so I suggested a *Droschke* that we should not be late. Off we drove and were at the theatre just before 6.30. No doors open, not a soul about, and I shall never forget the twinkle in your father's eyes as he said: Edith, what have you done? The door slowly opened and I tore up the steps to the second *Rang* where our box was. Suddenly I heard peals of laughter and looking round saw your father supporting himself against a pillar and with the others literally in fits of laughter. When at last he could speak he said: 'Infant, you will be the death of me'. We had an hour to wait in that box but I received an education from him. As each member of the orchestra came in he said: 'Now, Infant, that is So-and-so, listen to his tuning-up'.[2]

---

[1] Letter dated May 13 1883   [2] Letter dated December 25 1937

They also attended the rehearsals of the Gewandhaus Orchestra at nine in the morning, conducted by Carl Reinecke. Elgar was amazed that, except for the principals, the violinists played three to a desk. He was very impressed by Schumann's *Overture, Scherzo and Finale* — 'my ideal' he called Schumann in a letter to Buck.[1]

Five years later, in 1888, Elgar was to compose a *Suite in D* and the gavotte movement entitled *Contrasts: the Gavotte A.D. 1700 and 1900*, derives from an incident during this visit. Writing to Jaeger on February 4 1899 about it he says:

> I saw two dancers once in Leipzig who came down the stage in antique dress dancing a gavotte: when they reached the footlights they suddenly turned round & appeared to be two very young & modern people & danced a gay & lively measure: they had come down the stage *backwards* and danced away with their (modern) faces towards us — when they reached the back of the stage they suddenly turned round & the old, decrepit couple danced gingerly to the old tune.

∗   ∗   ∗

On December 16 1901 the Elgars left England to spend Christmas in Düsseldorf, travelling with A J Jaeger. They had been delayed by a cold of Alice's and by Elgar's recurring eye trouble. After a good journey and sea passage they arrived at 11.30 pm and were met by Professor Buths and his friend. In two days' time Buths was to conduct the first continental performance of *Gerontius*. They were taken to a comfortable house at 17, Ehrens Strasse. The next day they attended the first orchestral rehearsal with the soloists and met Ludwig Wüllner, who was to sing the part of Gerontius. The orchestra consisted of about 80 players and apparently (according to Jaeger) Elgar could find little fault with them, although the singer who was to take the part of the Angel left something to be desired. That evening there was a further rehearsal with the chorus. There was quite a considerable audience who had paid to hear the rehearsal and they applauded well.

The following morning there was another orchestral rehearsal, Elgar attending to the finer points of interpretation and then the performance in the evening. The weather was appalling, but the hall, which was superb accoustically, was full to capacity. The Elgars sat in the third row of the balcony and heard everything exceptionally well. After Part I, Elgar held a reception in the 'Soloisten-Zimmer',

---

[1] Letter dated July 1 1883

where he and Buths were congratulated by many musicians who had travelled from other towns for the performance. Elgar was enthusiastically called at the end. It took him a long time to reach the podium, but the applause never ceased. A large laurel wreath was handed to him and he had to ask Buths what to do with it! After the concert there was a supper, Elgar making a modest speech of thanks to Buths, Wüllner and Jaeger and eventually they drove back to their residence at 1.30 am.

Jaeger wrote the following letter to Dorabella about the performance on December 29:

> I never heard such intellectual deeply felt singing. Not that W's voice is wonderful. No! But his Brains & his heart are; & they are more than mere voice in a work of such greatness as this wonderful Gerontius. We were delighted & moved to tears. As for Mrs. E., you can imagine her state of seventh-heaven-beatitude, with eyebrow lifting, neck twisting, forget-me-not glances towards the invisible Heavens! Don't think I am making fun of her! I am not; but you know her signs of deep emotion over the Dr's music don't you?

The following day, Friday, the Elgars were invited to the home of the artist Carl Sohn. A number of painters and musicians had also been invited in order to meet Elgar and they spent three hours over dinner. On the Saturday, Elgar went to Cologne with Jaeger, Buths and E Johnstone (of the *Manchester Guardian*) to visit old Franz Wüllner, who was director of the Cologne Conservatoire and conductor of the Gürzenich Concerts. He promised to produce *Gerontius* as his first concert in the following year.

On December 29 the Elgars left for Mainz, where they stayed a couple of days, finally returning to London, having endured a very rough crossing on New Year's Day 1902. That night they stayed at the Langham Hotel and went to a Promenade Concert, returning home the next day.

* * *

The Elgars returned to Düsseldorf again with Jaeger and Rodewald on May 16 1902 in order to attend the Lower Rhine Music Festival. They arrived on the following day, having had 'a stuffy downstairs cabin'. The first concert of the festival, on the 18th, was Bach's *Mass in B Minor*, which they thought 'most splendid'. *Gerontius* was performed on the 20th, again with Wüllner and this time with Muriel Foster singing the part of the Angel. It was an excellent performance and Henry Wood, who was present, later wrote in his book *My Life of Music*:

Postcard sent by Alice Elgar to Carice from Düsseldorf, 1902.

Elgar was recalled 20 times after the end of the first part. I have never seen an audience so excited nor a composer so spontaneously acclaimed, certainly not an Englishman — unless, perhaps, Sullivan after the first performance of 'The Golden Legend'[1]

The Elgars were given two enormous laurel leaves tied with coloured ribbon. Printed in silver lettering on each ribbon were the words 'Niederrheinisches Musik Fest'. Alice was very proud of them and they were hung up in the study at 'Craeg Lea'. After the performance Elgar was to receive what he regarded as the most important compliment of his life up to that period. This came from Richard Strauss, who was to propose a toast after a luncheon party to 'the first progressive English musician, Meister Elgar'.

On May 22 they left Düsseldorf and travelled to Kassel, where there were 'beautiful trees and beech woods', staying for two nights at the Hotel Royal. They then continued their journey to see the birthplace of Bach at Eisenach, and the following day left for Dresden via Leipzig, where they stayed for the next three days at the Bellevue Hotel. Elgar and Rodewald visited the opera and the theatre here. On their way back to Eisenach they had to spend three hours in Leipzig. As it was very hot they decided to go to the Hotel Sedan, where Elgar had stayed during his first trip to Leipzig in 1882. On their return to Eisenach, Rodewald was unwell and the heat was unbearable. They travelled back to Düsseldorf to the Hotel Hausa on June 3. The entries in Alice's diary for that day read: 'horrid hot room' and 'heat fearful 94 in shade'. On the following day they left for England and after a good crossing arrived safely at the Langham Hotel.

* * *

In July 1902, Elgar went to Bayreuth with a friend, Mr Ramsden, arriving, having travelled via Mainz, on the 22nd. In six days they heard the entire *Ring* and *Parsifal*. When Elgar returned his thoughts turned to writing his oratorio *The Apostles*. As W H Reed says:

Who knows whether his witnessing the descent of the Holy Grail in *Parsifal* at Bayreuth did not stir his memory and bring again to the surface the words that made such an impression on him as far back as 1868, words spoken by Mr. Francis Reeve, who little dreamed of their significance.

The Apostles were poor men at the time of their calling; perhaps before the descent of the Holy Ghost not cleverer than some of you here.[2]

---

[1] pp324–5   [2] *Elgar*, p66

The form that *The Apostles* was to take, using *leitmotiv*, as in Wagner, was also probably decided on this visit. In any case, Elgar was roused to start work on his proposed 'trilogy' immediately he arrived home.

* * *

The Elgars travelled to Cologne on May 19 1904 for a performance of *The Apostles*, although Elgar had insisted to Jaeger that he didn't want to go. They had a good crossing and went straight to the Dom Hotel in Cologne. The next day they met Jaeger and went to the first rehearsal. Elgar was introduced to the chorus and given a good reception. On the 21st, however, some of the soloists did not turn up for the early rehearsal and Elgar was rather displeased. Nevertheless, after a rehearsal in the evening there was great applause. Elgar sent a postcard to Dorabella with a picture of the Gürzenich Concert Hall on the front. The following message was written all the way round it:

> I know you don't want this but I send it with much love. The Apostles comes off here tomorrow. Mosshead [ie, Jaeger] is here & Alice & I am very hot & want Bier. Yours Edw.d E.

The performance was a great success, with splendid playing by the 150-strong orchestra, and Elgar was called up on to the platform after Part I — a rare honour, according to Jaeger — and twice at the end. Alice wrote in her diary the following day: 'Much congratulation, the Moss quite pink with happiness. Very thankful.' Elgar made a speech that evening after supper. On the 26th they should have left for Düsseldorf but Elgar was unwell, with a chill and cough, and dare not travel. They left two days later, when he was much better, and visited an exhibition there which displayed 'very interesting and lovely pictures'. Next day they had an excellent crossing home, but a long, tiring journey to Victoria.

* * *

Elgar and Frank Schuster travelled to Mainz on November 29 1904 for a performance of *The Apostles* given the following day and conducted by Fritz Volbach. It was another success, Alice, writing in her usual impassioned way: 'It was said there had never been such a triumph in Mainz D.G.' On December 1 they travelled from Mainz to Rotterdam, where they stayed at the Maas Hotel. A further performance of *The Apostles* was given here the following day and then they went on to The Hague before travelling to Cologne. On the 7th they visited Düsseldorf, where they had lunch with Professor Buths.

101

In Brussels, on their way back home, they saw *La Vie Parisienne*, arriving home safely on the 9th, Alice meeting them in London at 7 pm.

* * *

At the end of 1910 the Elgars travelled on December 13th to Krefeld, which Alice thought was a 'depressing looking place'. They booked in at the Künstter Zimmer Hotel, but disliked it intensely — 'horrible gas stove — room covered with pictures all dingy and soiled looking'. Elgar was horrified by it and so Alice persuaded him to wait there until she went to see the Krefelder Hof Hotel. This was much more suited to their taste and so they moved. Elgar was to conduct a performance of the *First Symphony* on Saturday December 17. The orchestral rehearsal on the previous Thursday cheered him after the unpromising start with their accommodation. The concert itself was most successful. Alice's diary reads: 'Great performance of Symphony. Immense enthusiasm & impression. E. recalled again & again'. They left Krefeld the day after the performance and lunched with Professor Buths in Düsseldorf, returning home on Monday, December 19.

Bavaria

In the summer of 1892 the Elgars were taken to Bavaria by Minnie Baker of 'Hasfield Court'. They left Dover on Monday July 25 and crossed to Ostend, then continued their journey by train to Malines and thence to the Hotel du Nord in Cologne. Before leaving Cologne on the following day, they visited the cathedral and then travelled via Bonn, where they visited Beethoven's birthplace, to Mainz, staying overnight at the Hotel Englischer Hof. They arrived at Bayreuth on the 27th and went to 7, Ludwig Strasse, where they were to stay. During their visit the party went to hear *Tristan, Die Meistersinger* and *Parsifal* (twice). After leaving Bayreuth they journeyed as far as Nuremberg, staying at the Shlenk's Hotel. Here the houses and graves of Albert Dürer and Hans Sachs were visited. Travelling via Munich, where they went to a performance of *Cavalleria Rusticana*, they eventually arrived in the quieter mountains of Bavaria. From Obersdorf, in the Allgäuer Alps, Elgar wrote to his Grafton nephews and nieces:

> We are now in a little village all among mountains upon which (some of them) high up in the clouds there is snow lying: & it looks very wonderful to see. Now all the houses in this little town are built of wood! & have balconies running round in which the people, in this hot weather, have their meals & sit in the evening. This is the end of the railway — the mountains will not let it go any further & it is very strange to be here as no-one speaks English & we are the only English people anywhere about (Sud Bayern. August 8th)

Elgar spent a great deal of time noting all the local folklore, examining the Bavarian architecture, both domestic and ecclesiastical, for the Catholic churches and wayside shrines were immensely interesting to him. They continued their journey on to Garmisch, staying at a pension called the Villa Bader owned by an English couple, Mr and Mrs Slingsby Bethell, and then they returned home via Lindau and Heidelberg, where they stayed at the Schloss Hotel. Here Elgar asked Minnie to post some of *The Black Knight*, on which he had been working during the holiday, to Novellos, to bring him luck. Longfellow was a favourite poet of Elgar's mother and from Heidelberg he wrote a letter to her describing the torch-light procession of some students:

> I must send a line from *here* about which we have read & thought so much ... it did remind me of Hyperion & the beer scandal etc. etc.

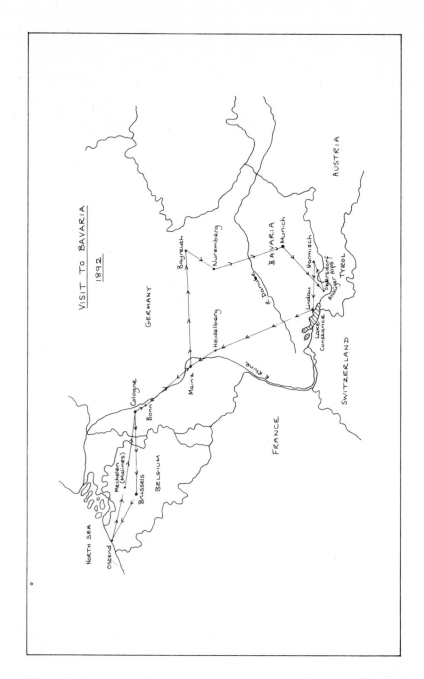

VISIT TO BAVARIA
1892

NORTH SEA

Ostend

Mechelen
(Malines)

Brussels

BELGIUM

Cologne

Bonn

Mainz

R. Rhine

GERMANY

Heidelberg

Bayreuth

Nuremberg

R. Danube

BAVARIA

Munich

Garmisch

Oberstdorf
Allgauer Alps

Lindau

Lake
Constance

SWITZERLAND

FRANCE

TYROL

AUSTRIA

104

Villa Bader, Garmisch.

From Heidelberg they travelled to Cologne, where the next day they were able to take part in the High Mass at Cologne Cathedral before continuing on to the Hotel d'Europe in Brussels. On Monday August 15 they returned to London, having thoroughly enjoyed their trip. Elgar was 'fired with songs' and set to work with renewed vigour.

* * *

The Elgars returned to Bavaria in 1893. Minnie Baker, who had accompanied them in the previous year, looked after Carice. They had hoped to let 'Forli', their house in Malvern, for the summer, but the plan fell through, so they packed the family plate into a chest and it was looked after by Basil Nevinson. On August 2 they travelled down to Dover and stayed overnight at the Castle Hotel. The following day they had a rough crossing to Ostend, then continued by rail to Cologne, where they stayed at the Hotel du Nord. Their journey to Garmisch took them via Mainz and Munich. They arrived at Garmisch on August 5 and stayed at the Villa Bader again for the next fortnight.

Both Elgar and Alice took great pleasure in their surroundings, Elgar writing in his diary notes on the cows coming home with their bells, the oxen drawing wagons, the native costumes, the occupations of the villagers — 'Old man in village with immense heap of fir trimmings solemnly chopping of (sic) green ends & making two heaps — one of wood & the other of green shoots'; the construction of the houses — complete with a drawing of a wooden balcony — and even how the tea was made. He relaxed completely, played cricket and thoroughly enjoyed himself. Their one disappointing trip was to Oberammergau on the 13th, which they found expensive but enjoyed seeing the local woodcarving and paying a visit to the theatre.

On August 17 they had to leave Garmisch to return to Munich for the Musikfest. Here they met Rosa Burley, the Malvern headmistress, and her pupil Alice Davey, who had found rooms for them at 13 Glückstrasse. That evening they went to a performance of *Die Meistersinger* at the vast Hoftheatre, where the operas were staged. During the next two weeks they also saw the whole of *The Ring, Tannhäuser, Tristan und Isolde* and *Die Feen*. Elgar was greatly amused by some of the incidents in the operas:

> ... he was immensely tickled by the all-too-generous proportions of the Rhinemaidens and, I think, always hoped that the ropes which supported them would give way. The unathletic gods, with the terrible clubs which they clumped on the stage, also pleased him, as did the final moment when Levi [ie. Herman Levi, the conductor] tottered on to the stage, a small stiff figure leading a vast soprano.[1]

It was clear that Elgar intended to enjoy everything that Munich could offer, including the black beer, the sausages and naturally the famous buildings — the Church of the Theatines, the Pinakothek galleries, the rococo decoration of the Nymphenburg Palace and, of course, the superb Hoftheatre itself. During one of his afternoons of exploration he took a horse-tram (which ran until midnight) to go to the end of the route. He asked for the 'letzte Ruhe-Platz' (literally 'the last resting place'), only to find that he had been put down at a cemetery! After the opera performances they would adjourn at the Hofbräuhaus, where discussions of the performance took place. Elgar took a great many notes on what he heard. Before leaving Munich he bought a picture of Wagner.

---

[1] *Edward Elgar, the record of a friendship*, Rosa Burley, pp 64–5

On September 3 the Elgars had to leave to make their way home via Cologne and Ostend, so that Elgar could play (for the last time) in the orchestra of The Three Choirs Festival.

*   *   *

In 1894 the Elgars left Carice with Rosa Burley, setting off for their holiday in Bavaria on July 31 and arriving the next day at the Hook of Holland. Travelling via Munich they arrived at Garmisch on 3 August and were met by John Slingsby Bethell, who escorted them to the Villa Bader. Much of the holiday was spent walking to their favourite spots. The entry in Alice's diary for the 5th reads: 'A's boots first appeared at Garmisch'. Elgar also played golf. In the local inn, 'Die drei Mohren', they saw the Tyrolean *Schuplättl* dancers which had a profound effect on Elgar and were later to influence his Bavarian Highlands music. For four days they were joined by Isobel and Hilda Fitton and their mother, close friends from Malvern. On August 15 the Elgars left by train for Innsbruck, where they stayed at the Hotel d'Europe. Elgar was much impressed by his surroundings. A diary note reads: 'Much new snow on mountains. E. wildly rushing after engines. Lovely effect of sun setting. Lights in snow and distant peaks'. On the Sunday they watched the 'Procession of the Blessed Sacrament' through the village. Elgar made a note of the bell-chimes:

They returned to Garmisch and the weather at first became really hot — 'too hot to do anything'. At Partenkirchen, Elgar bought Alice a cowbell bracelet which she thought 'quite lovely'. He played football with the Slingsby-Bethell boys and when the weather turned wet indulged in such pastimes as charades and musical chairs. On September 13 they left Garmisch for the Hotel Bahnhof Garnie in Munich, in order to hear performances of Wagner's *Götterdämmerung* and *Die Meistersinger*. Returning home, they stayed overnight at Frankfurt, where they saw Goethe's house and at Bruges, where they visited the cathedral, including the belfry. They had a beautiful crossing from Ostend and arrived home on the 21st.

As a result of these holidays in Bavaria, Alice and Edward collaborated intimately together on a series of six part-songs entitled *From the Bavarian Highlands*. Before her marriage Alice had published poetry and had a certain flair in this respect, although she could not be described as a great poet. The six poems written by Alice were carefully revised by them both. They centred on two adjoining villages in Bavaria, Garmisch and Partenkirchen, which lie below the Zugspitze, the highest peak in the Bavarian Alps, and which, over the last three years, the Elgars had grown to love.

The first is called *The Dance* and refers to Sonnenbichl, near Garmisch, on the northern side and in sight of the Zugspitze. No. 2, *False Love*, is subtitled *Wamberg*, a village on the western side of Garmisch. No. 3, *Lullaby*, has as its subtitle 'Near Hammersbach', south of Garmisch. The inspiration for the fourth song, *Aspiration*, was the pilgrim's chapel of St Anton near Partenkirchen. Behind the village a pinewood path leads to the chapel built in 1734, with its pink and white cupola and pink and silver interior. *On the Alm* is the title of No. 5; *Hoch Alp*, meaning 'High Alp', is added, the one referred to being south of Hammersbach. An alm is a mountain pasture, where in the summer a girl would live in a hut to tend the grazing cattle. Years later the sound of cowbells heard in this landscape were to appear in Elgar's score for *The Starlight Express*. The sixth song is *The Marksman*, which describes a shooting club on the Staffelsee. This was a happy partnership between husband and wife and the song-cycle was finally completed on April 9 1895. *From the Bavarian Highlands* was dedicated to the proprietors of the Garmisch pension, Mr and Mrs Henry Slingsby Bethell, and was accepted for publication in December of that year.

*   *   *

A few months after the completion of the song-cycle, the Elgars left for another Bavarian holiday on July 31 1895, making the channel crossing from Dover to Ostend and then travelling on to Bruges. After a couple of days here visiting the places of interest, they journeyed through Germany via Cologne, Würzburg, which was — 'very fine, & City all beflagged for military fete', Regensburg and Passau. Here they boarded a boat and sailed down the Danube to Linz, which, according to Alice's diary, was 'very nice only to (sic) cold & blowing'. The next day (9th August) they took a train to Salzburg, where they stayed at the Hotel am Stein. The Elgars thought Salzburg 'lovely' and travelled on the cable railway and visited Mozart's house. On the 12th they left for Berchtesgaden but didn't like their hotel room and were still dissatisfied after changing to another. The weather was wet, and having been soaked in the thunderstorm they were damp and wretched. A visit to the salt-works was spoiled for Alice by the

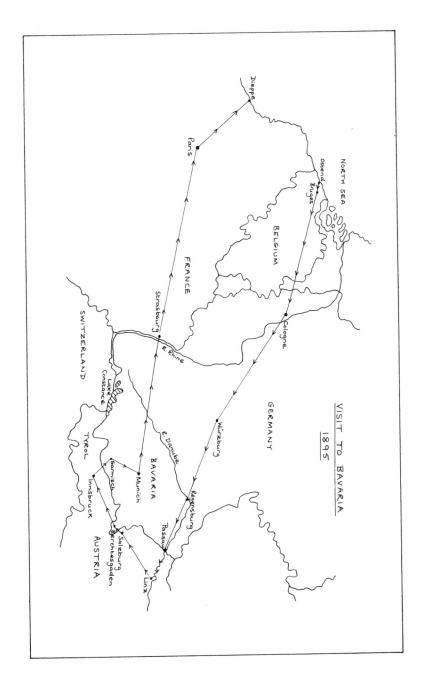

VISIT TO BAVARIA
1895

109

costume she was made to wear and which she found 'too repellent'. Their journey continued on the 17th, when they left for Innsbruck, and three days later had a lovely drive from Innsbruck to Garmisch, lunching on the way at Mittenwald. They arrived at Garmisch about 5.30 pm, and that evening attended a fancy ball.

For some reason Alice did not keep her diary for the next ten days and it is therefore impossible to know how they spent their days, although it is reasonable to assume that the time was passed visiting their usual haunts. At the beginning of September, however, the weather was very hot and on the afternoon of the 3rd an 'Elgar benefit' cricket match was organised and a tea-party held at the Bethell pension. The following morning, after touching farewells from the Bethells, the Elgars left for Munich. Elgar obtained tickets for the opera *Der Fliegende Holländer* that evening, but they did not think it was very well done. On the way home they stayed in Strasbourg at the Hotel Terminus for two nights, but Elgar, who was suffering from throat trouble, had to have the doctor and was given arrowroot. Then they returned via Paris and their much loved Hotel des deux Mondes, spending a good deal of time in the Louvre and visiting Notre Dame. On September 11, a 'lovely day', they took the ferry from Dieppe and arrived in London about 7 pm.

* * *

There was no holiday in Bavaria in 1896 but on August 10 1897 the Elgars returned once again. They docked at Flushing and then travelled via Cologne to Munich. Here on the 12th they went to a performance of Wagner's *Tristan und Isolde* and met Richard Strauss. The next day they went on to Garmisch, staying once again with their friends the Slingsby Bethells. All their old haunts were re-visited — Partenkirchen, Hammersbach and so on. Elgar was busy with his camera, photographing the mountain thunderstorms and the family outside the pension. On September 1 they left Garmisch to return to Munich, where that evening they met Strauss again and went to a performance of *Don Giovanni* at the Residency Theatre. The following evening they saw *Der Fliegende Holländer*. Their return journey took them again via Cologne and they arrived safely back in London on September 6. This was to be their last Bavarian holiday.

The first performance of *From the Bavarian Highlands* took place at Worcester on April 21 1896 in its original version for four-part chorus and piano accompaniment. Later that year Elgar wrote an alternative orchestral accompaniment, and in 1897 set numbers 1, 3 and 6 for orchestra alone, which were entitled *Three Bavarian Dances*, comprising *The Cance, Lullaby* and *The Marksman*.

From the Bavarian Highlands.

SIX CHORAL SONGS
(S.A.T.B.)

with accompaniment for

PIANO

(or Orchestra)

The words imitated from Bavarian Volkslieder and Schnadahüpfler,
by C. ALICE ELGAR.
The Music composed
by

EDWARD ELGAR.

Op 27.

	Tonic Sol-fa	Old Notation			Tonic Sol-fa	Old Notation
Nº1. The Dance.	4ᴰ	9ᴰ	Nº4. Aspiration.		3ᶜ	6ᴰ
Nº2 False Love.	3ᶜ	9ᴰ	Nº5 On the Alm.		3ᴰ	9ᴰ
Nº3. Lullaby.	3ᶜ	9ᶜ	Nº6. The Marksman.		6ᴰ	1/0

Tonic Sol-fa (Complete) 1/6 net   Vocal Score (Complete) 6/6 net
N.B. An edition of this work is published for Male Voice Choirs, arranged
by LESLIE WOODGATE
Prices: Nos. 1, 2, 3, & 5. 6d. net each. No. 4, 4d. net No. 6. 1/- net

Orchestral parts may be had on hire.

JOSEPH WILLIAMS
London

Made and printed in Great Britain.

Italy

The Elgars travelled to the Italian Riviera on November 25 1903 for the winter months. It was Elgar's first visit to Italy. Carice was still at school, but at the end of term came out to her parents with Rosa Burley. Alice and Edward travelled via Calais, Paris — where they had time to visit the Louvre — and Marseilles. On the 28th they arrived at the coastal resort of Bordighera. Alice wrote in her diary: 'Arrived at Bordighera all safely. D. G. Nice room at Hotel Royal. Rather depressing at dinner, large nearly empty room with not very enchanting people'. The weather was poor and Bordighera itself seemed too English for Elgar — the roads were full of English nursery maids, old women and children, as in Malvern. Although the view appealed to him, he wrote to Frank Schuster on December 8:

> I want something more Italian *more civilised* & would prefer to be virtuous at Alassio or wildly wicked at Monte Carlo to being betwixt and between here ...

On the same letter he goes on to relate a day with a donkey which Alice thought 'one of the most lovely days':

> ... Alice & I have been out *with a donkey* all day up in the woods & mountains — donkey's name is 'Grisia' — a lovely beast ... Bought some figs today — did not know name so asked for 'frutti, per habilimenti d'Adam ed Eva'. I got 'em ... Oh! that donkey. She's a love. I am going to buy her & ride her from here to Alassio! ... We are both riotously well & shall never come home. We go to Alassio on Thursday.

They had visited Alassio, further down the coast, earlier in the week to choose a villa, settling on the Villa San Giovanni on the hillside behind the station and next to the English Church. The villa is built of irregular stone blocks with red brick surrounding the doors and shuttered windows, and with three large brick archways across the front. The large lounge, with two French windows overlooking the front garden, has a beautiful curved ceiling and marble fireplace. There is also a spacious dining room and kitchen. Two flights of marble staircase lead to the bathroom on the landing and the four rooms on the upper floor. A balcony on this floor offers a wonderful views over the Mediterranean. After leaving Bordighera on December 10 the Elgars slept the first night in Alassio at the Salisbury Hotel and went to the villa the next day. It was pouring with rain and, although they found the servants busy, the house was dreadfully cold, the wood

Photograph taken by Elgar of Alice and Carice Elgar, with Rosa Burley, on the Roman Bridge at Alassio.

Villa San Giovanni, Alassio.

was damp and there was no stove alight. Elgar had arranged to hire a piano which was eventually delivered by 12 men, hired by the station master, all sweating and swearing as they staggered with it up to the villa and then up the two flights of stairs! Nevertheless, that day they managed to get Elgar's study arranged. Elgar liked the house, the Italian servants and the high terraced garden with its lemons, olives and flowers. Writing to Jaeger he says:

> This place is jolly — real Italian & no nursemaids calling out *'Now, Master Johnny!'* — like that anglicised paradise Bordighera! pff!
>
> Our cook is an angel: do come out — it seems *so easy* to come & so difficult to go back — & have a meal or two. What matters the Mediterranean being rough and grey? What matters rain in torrents? Who cares for gales? *Tramontana*? We have such meals! Such wine! Gosh!
>
> It is curious burning nothing but olive wood in the open fires — they bring a load with a corresponding number of *fir cones* (dry) for fire lighters — no smoke — no dust — paradise. We are at last living a life. The Mosquitoes are a trial & I am stung because I refused to believe in 'em & wd. not pull down the mosquito curtains at night round my bed.[1]

Eventually, although at first they had to wrap themselves in fur-lined cloaks at night, the house became warmer. Elgar bought some music-paper and began orchestrating two part-songs, *The Snow* and *Fly Singing Bird*. A number of cats frequented the garden and sat in pairs on the garden seat. Elgar suspended a large jug in an enormous Caruba tree over the seat, with a string attached, so that he could look up from his work and drench them. He also made a catapult and fired at them with old shoes he had picked up in the garden! For another week the weather remained wretched, but on December 20 they had a lovely day walking by the sea and watching the ships. The next day Rosa Burley and Carice arrived at Milan and the following day were met by the Elgars at Genoa. They stayed the night and the following morning, according to Rosa Burley's book, Elgar found a music shop and bought some orchestral manuscript paper, although he had purchased some earlier. Her description of the hiring of the piano at this time, however, appears to be suspect, for according to Alice's diary it had been hired and installed 12 days before. On Christmas Eve they all went to the Midnight Mass at a little inland church for the ceremony of the blessing of the lamb. All the local shepherds were present and Elgar greatly enjoyed this experience.

---

[1] Letter dated January 13 1903

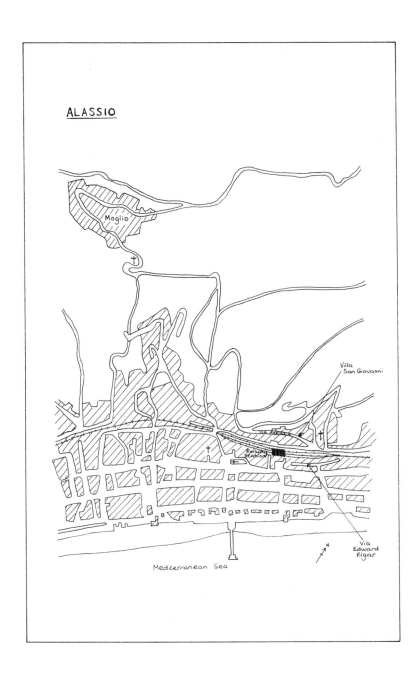

ALASSIO

Moglio

Villa San Giovanni

Via Ferrara

Railway Station

Via Edward Elgar

N

Mediterranean Sea

From the balcony outside his study he enjoyed watching the fishermen still drawing in their nets in the same way as had been described by Virgil. He was also delighted to see the unloading of wine from Sardinia for a local trattoria, and refused to drink anything else. The Italian countryside lived up to all their expectations and Elgar's greatest love was walking on the hillsides among the olive groves, with spectacular views below of Alassio and the Mediterranean. One day on the hills he met Dr J Armitage Robinson, the Dean of Westminster, and they walked back together. He visited them the following day and returned again for lunch a few days later.

Elgar had hoped to start work on a symphony here, but the constant bad weather and cold winds depressed him and he felt no inspiration for composition. In a letter to Jaeger on January 3 his tone had changed from his earlier correspondence:

> This visit has been, is, artistically a complete *failure* and I can do nothing ... The symphony will not be written in this sunny (?) land. You must understand that when a wind does come — and it is apparently *always* on — it is no bearable kindly east wind of England — but a tearing, piercing, lacerating *devil* of a wind: one step outside the door & I am cut in two, numbed & speechless: I have never regretted anything more than this horribly disappointing journey: wasting time, money & temper. Our house *is* comfortable & there is a decent library here. Carice is here — Miss Burley brought her — & we are all happy together & only want weather!

However, on January 9 it was a lovely day and after lunch the Elgars caught the train to Andora. Here they saw the oil being manufactured from the local grown olives, went to the Roman Bridge, watched a shepherd with his flock of sheep and eventually reached San-Michele del Colle. This visit was to prove a great inspiration to Elgar. Instead of the proposed symphony, he worked on a concert overture which he called *In the South* for the forthcoming Elgar Festival to be held at Covent Garden on March 14–16 of that year. It became, however, more of a symphonic poem than an overture. Although the opening theme, suggesting George Sinclair's bulldog Dan in a fight, had previously been written, Elgar said that his idea for the overture came from the 'thoughts and sensations of one beautiful afternoon in the Vale of Andora'. The opening suggests the mountains and flowers and also the 'wine and macaroni' according to Elgar's letters to Percy Pitt regarding the festival programme notes. On the manuscript he wrote some lines from 'The Daisy' by Tennyson, which sum up the atmosphere of the region:

What hours were thine and mine
In lands of palm and southern pine
In lands of palm, of orange blossom
Of olive, aloe, and maize and vine.

In one section Elgar captures the essence of past Roman glories, influenced by his visit to the Roman Bridge, imagining the 'grand relentless force which made its way through and endured'. This time he quotes on the manuscript words from Byron's *Childe Harold*:

... a land
Which was the mightiest in its old command
And *is* the lovliest ...
Wherein were cast ...
... the men of Rome!
Thou art the garden of the world.

A certain three-note phrase in the work was suggested by the village of Moglio, which clings spectacularly to the hillside above the town of Alassio. The Elgars would often walk as far as the church by the old mule track. The tiny houses are built below the level of the steep *salitas*, however, and the inhabitants, after walking down the hillside, suddenly disappear from view. Rosa Burley, in *Edward Elgar: the record of a friendship*, says:

Edward loved this and never tired of seeing them disappear.
'There one really could roll home', someone said.
'Moglio, Moglio roglio roglio, said Edward with a pleasing access of fatuity.[1]

He set the name to music and repeated it many times:

Mo - gli - o Mo - gli - o _____

One day, again according to Rosa Burley, they came to a tiny ruined chapel built like a classic temple by a group of pine trees. Suddenly, a shepherd dressed in sheepskin appeared from behind the chapel, driving his flock before him. Although it is not clear whether this was the shepherd they watched at Andora, it was this incident which gave rise to the 'Canto Popolare' theme for solo viola, which, however, was Elgar's own composition, not an Italian folk-song.

---

[1] p 170

CONCERT-OVERTURE
IN THE SOUTH
(ALASSIO)
BY
EDWARD ELGAR
OP. 50.

Dedicated to Frank Schuster, the overture was well received at its first performance on March 16. One report of the time is quoted by W H Reed:

> We account 'In the South' to be a really great and beautiful creation. Much was, of course, to be expected from such a composer when paying a first fascinating visit to Italy, but it was not certain that the outcome of contact with such a land would also be fascinating. Yet so it is.
>
> The fresh feeling of gladness; the gentle and musing melancholy which comes of contemplating exquisite scenes of nature; the energy which thoughts of a great heroic past develop — all are here in rich abundance, and best of all is the artistic restraint that controlled the musicians' thick-coming fancies and made his whole powers minister to the beauty without which music is no better than a tinkling cymbal.[1]

Although they had intended to stay longer, probably another month, the weather turned cold again and Elgar was forbidden by a doctor to drink any more Sardinian wine, so they decided to return home. As well as the climatic disappointments, Elgar had received a letter on January 21 from Sir W Carrington, asking him to dine at Malborough House on February 3 and meet the King. He was anxious to return home to finish his work and so on January 30 they left for Marseilles. After staying overnight at the Hotel Terminus they travelled through France the following day and on February 1 arrived at Calais before having a beautiful crossing home.

The villa where the Elgars stayed, and which was built specifically for tourists, is now re-named Villa Tiziana, but the house and garden appear to have changed little since the turn of the century. The fine Caruba tree is still standing — (apparently a local species of the Carob) and fruit trees still abound in the terraced garden. Along the seafront the Edwardian hotels, now gaily colour-washed, present a pleasing sight from the tiny pier. In the town itself, near the station, Alassio has honoured its one-time guest by naming a small street Via Edward Elgar.

*   *   *

For the first two months of 1907 the Elgars went to Italy again, leaving England on January 1. Before their visit Lady Elgar had written in December to Alfred Littleton of Novellos: 'We feel we must

---

[1] Elgar, p 79

give up our Italian journey ... we cannot undertake it without financial anxiety'. Eight days later, however, Elgar wrote to him: 'The
doctor insists on rest. Will you be so good as to send me some money'.
They sailed via Gibraltar, where they had wonderful views of the
Rock, and then on to Marseilles. Unfortunately the weather became
rough and the ship's doctor had to be called to attend to a cyst which
Elgar had developed. They journeyed with Canon Gorton, who was
acting British chaplain on Capri. On January 6 they arrived at Naples,
where they stayed at the Parker's Hotel. Alice found Naples dirty,
especially the Via Roma, but they explored the museums and took
a trip to Pompeii and were joined by Frank Schuster on the 9th. From
Naples they went on to Sorrento, but Alice was 'not much struck with
it'. Her diary for that day reads: '*Horrid* being shoved into boat
crowded with people & luggage, *hateful.*' On arrival at Capri, however, they liked the hotel and the island. Elgar went almost immediately to have his hair cut and discovered that the clients passed the time
while waiting for their turn with music. Not to be outdone, Elgar composed an *Andantino for violin, mandolin and guitar*, dated June 15
1907, for the general benefit. It was subtitled 'For the Barbers', but

'Via Edward Elgar'.

it did, however, remain incomplete. He was pleased to visit Dr Axel Munthe's beautiful villa, but the weather was wet and cold and he was constantly unwell with his throat.

For many days Elgar wondered whether or not to return home but could not come to a final decision. On February 7, Alice wrote in desperation: 'What to do?' However, at the last moment they decided to continue and sailed for Rome on the 12th. From the start they loved the city — 'Rome beginning to impress us deeply', Alice wrote. They went to Mass at a church in the Piazza del Popolo and afterwards attended a concert where they met the Italian composer Sgambati. Perosi also called on them and, being a priest as well as a musician offered to show them around the Vatican. They also visited St Peter's, the many museums, drove down the Via Appia and were impressed with it all.

In Rome, Elgar composed the four unaccompanied part-songs Opus 53, to words by Tennyson, Byron, Shelley and Elgar himself: *There is sweet music, Deep in my soul, O Wild West Wind* and *Owls.* These were written as a result of Elgar's connection with the Morecambe Festival and his deep respect for the fine choirs of the north of England. *There is sweet music* he dedicated to Canon Gorton, and *Deep in my soul* to Mrs Julia Worthington, a wealthy American whom the Elgars had first met on their visit to the States two years earlier. The dedicatee of *O Wild West Wind* was Dr W G McNaught, a musician who often took part in the Madresfield Festival. *Owls* was dedicated to Pietro d'Alba, Carice's pet rabbit.

On February 23 they left Rome by train for the return journey which proved to be quite beautiful, with snow on the mountains and even deeper snow in the valleys. At 5.30 am on the 25th they arrived in Paris and after a short break at the Grand Hotel, continued at 9.50 am on a further train to the coast. They had a splendid crossing and the next day returned to Plâs Gwyn, their home in Hereford, where they were greeted by Carice and May Grafton.

* * *

On November 5 1907, obviously much impressed by their visit earlier in the year, the Elgars decided to return to Rome for the winter months, this time taking Carice and May with them. They let Plâs Gwyn to Captain and Mrs Inglefield and travelled by train via London, Paris and Genoa, arriving in Rome on the 7th. Here they rented 38a Via Gregoriana, a seven-roomed flat on the third floor of the building, from Mrs Dawes Rose, taking the accommodation for exactly five months. The view from the flat over the roof-tops to St Peter's was magnificent and they were able to watch some beautiful sunsets. Alice made arrangements to hire a cook and maids and Elgar hired a piano with Sgambati's help and two days after their arrival began taking French lessons at the Berlitz school. They were entertained at the British Embassy by the American composer John Alden Carpenter. Carice started Italian lessons and also took some singing lessons. Alice and May spent time visiting the shops trying to find Elgar some puzzles. They went to see *Tosca, Madame Butterfly* and *Die Meistersinger*, but found this strange in Italian dress. Elgar especially enjoyed the food and the wine.

At the beginning of the holiday Elgar worked on two part-songs: *A Christmas Greeting* to Alice's words, which he dedicated to G R Sinclair and the Hereford Cathedral choristers and finished on December 8, and *The Reveille*, with words by Bret Harte, which was for the Blackpool Musical Festival of 1908 and which he completed on December 26. This he dedicated to Henry Embleton, conductor of the Leeds Choral Society. Elgar wrote to Schuster at Christmas: 'This is my *Mecca & I love it all*'. On Christmas Day, however, they received bad news of May's father, William Grafton. In the New Year it was necessary for May to return home when it was obvious that her father was dying.

After the completion of the part-songs Elgar had started work on his *First Symphony*, but he found it very noisy working in Rome. He sent Alfred Littleton a postcard of the Via Appia on which he quoted the first three bars of the melody and stated 'This is it'. However, he told him that he doubted the work would be finished: 'I can't tell how much I shall be able to work here: there are "voices most vociferous" and pianos most pianiferous in the street which is otherwise quiet.'

Towards the end of January, Julia Worthington came to Rome and Elgar went to the theatre with her, but at the beginning of February he went down with an attack of influenza which caused Alice some worry. On March 13 they went to a party at the Hotel Bristol arranged by American friends. Singers from the Sistine Chapel were engaged to perform, but Elgar found their singing rather disappointing.

Sgambati showed him the various possessions given to him by Liszt:

> The first copy of the score of 'Siegfried Idyll' sent by Wagner to Liszt in Rome with a little writing on the title. Also the *first* exemplar of *Faust* (Berlioz) sent by B. to Liszt! & above all (1868) the full score of *Meistersinger* sent by W. to L. with words & title 'De profundis clamavi!' at the top, a date etc. below & *Richard*'.

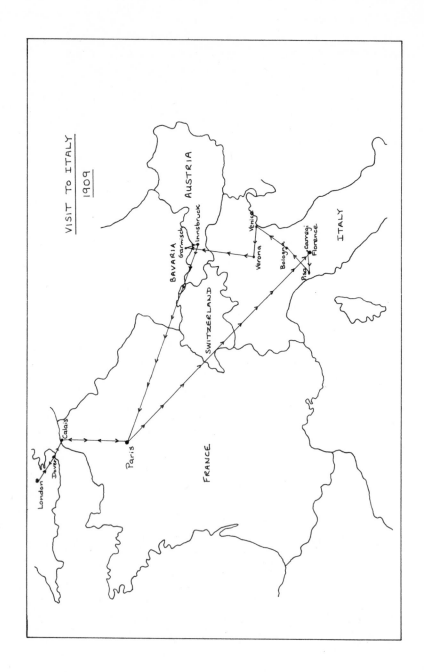

VISIT TO ITALY
1909

'How wonderful to see & touch', he wrote to Jaeger on April 26.

In April there was a two-day national strike. The funeral of an Italian workman on April 2 was used as a socialist demonstration. There was some shooting in the Piazza di Gesù by the police and lives were lost. Elgar and Carice visited the scene again later and Elgar described it in a letter to May Grafton:

> Bright sun that a.m. found the streets occupied in every direction with troops, bayonets & loaded rifles ... It was wonderful to walk over that great empty square with soldiers ready for the fray all round. And all the horses of the cavalry picketed on one side.

But it was Holy Week that was the highlight of this visit to Rome for Alice. On Good Friday she took Carice to St Sylvester's to hear Father Bernard Vaughan preach and on Easter Sunday they went to the service at St Peter's. However, on this occasion they were disappointed. They had poor seats and did not find the ceremonial either beautiful or impressive.

The Elgars began their return voyage by ship on May 8, eventually reaching Plymouth on the 15th and docking at Tilbury the following day. It had been a fascinating and illuminating holiday for Elgar. He had sketched some music to accompany a procession of Italian nobles and ladies of past days. Eventually this music, improvised on his holiday, was to become the basis of the *Coronation March* written for the Coronation of King George V in June 1911. In a letter to Walford Davies, Elgar stated that he had been greatly interested in Rome and wished very much to return, but continued, 'I could not reconstruct the ancient period or the renaissance: I could only efface the present by peopling the place with folk living from 1650 to 1800. Evelyn, Horace Walpole etc. etc. I felt a classic failure but learned much & want to learn more.'[1]

* * *

In April 1909 the Elgars returned to Italy for a holiday with Julia ('Pippa') Worthington. Elgar went on ahead to Paris for a week on the 9th,[2] Alice and Carice meeting him there on the 17th. The next day they went to High Mass at La Madeleine and Pippa met them on the 19th. After another night at the Hotel des deux Mondes they left Paris for the journey to Florence. Pippa had a rented villa, called the Villa Silli, at Carregi, a long drive out of Florence opposite Fiesole. They stayed here from April 21 to May 28, being joined by Rosa

---

[1] Letter dated July 15 1908   [2] See p 89

Burley and Frank Schuster for a few days at the end of April. Whilst here they heard a concert conducted by Mascagni. Sadly they received news of the death of Jaeger on May 18.

Naturally they were greatly impressed by Florence and bought a book about it. Alice was charmed by the butterflies, flowers and lizards but found the black ants terrifying. She wrote from the villa to Alice Stuart-Wortley:

> My dearest Namesake,
>   I have been wanting to send you a few lines from this lovely place and to tell you that Edward is looking well and rested. I trust you will hear E's impressions tonally some day.

The result of this visit was two part-songs, *Angelus* (*Tuscany*) (Opus 56) and *Go Song of Mine* (Opus 57), perhaps his finest work for unaccompanied choir. The first was dedicated to Alice Stuart-Wortley and the latter to Alfred Littleton. There is also an existing sketch-book which is headed 'Opera in Three Acts — Edward Elgar — Carregi', and another sketch-book bought in Florence which contains a stage set. He also made some sketches for the *Violin Concerto*.

After leaving Carregi they drove to Pisa, with which they were much impressed, and then went on to Bologna before arriving in Venice, where they stayed for the next eight days at the Hotel Regina. The weather was glorious but a little too hot for sight-seeing. They did, however, enjoy their trip in a gondola. In Venice, Elgar began making sketches of what was to become his *Second Symphony*. In his sketch-book X (1909) Elgar wrote: 'I wish I could get the (1000000) frogs in the Vineyard into the score of Sym. II — a fine sound. Aristophanes etc.' He got up at 5 o'clock to see the beauty of Venice without people. According to Sanford Terry, at one point he had it in his mind to use the contrast between the interior of St Mark's at Venice and the sunlit and lively Piazza outside as a representation of the opening subjects of the slow movement and scherzo, but later he apparently gave up this idea.

They left Venice on June 7 with Pippa but then parted company and travelled on to Verona and then to Garmisch. At Garmisch they went to see the Strausses before starting their return journey home, travelling via Innsbruck and Paris, where they returned for the night to the Hotel de deux Mondes. On the 16th they left for England and had a perfectly calm crossing — Alice's diary reads: 'D. G. for safe return — & beautiful days'.

* * *

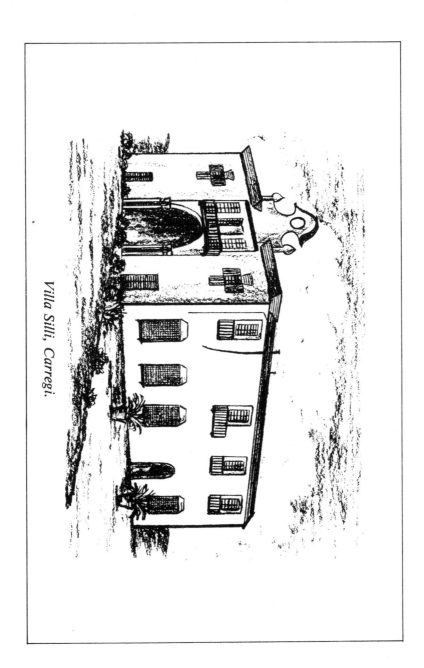

Villa Silli, Carregi.

127

('Go Song of Mine' (extract)

(*Careggi*, 1909.)

(11)

129

During the month of October 1911, Elgar went to Turin to conduct some of his own works. The orchestra was Toscanini's and the concerts were held during the International Exhibition on October 18 and 20. Included in the programmes were Weber's *Euryanthe* overture, Mozart's G minor Symphony and Mendelssohn's *Ruy Blas*. The Elgar works were *Enigma Variations*, the March from *Caractacus, Introduction and Allegro for String Orchestra*, the slow movement of the *Second Symphony*, the Prelude to *Gerontius* and the *Violin Concerto*. The soloist for the concert was Zakharevich, who at the age of 12 had played Tchaikovsky's concerto under the composer's baton.

* * *

In January 1913 Elgar was unwell and his doctor advised a trip abroad, Elgar decided to go alone to San Remo and had actually got his ticket, but both he and Alice were dejected about the idea. Alice's diary for January 30th records: 'E. very depressed at going to Riviera, said in car "If only we cd. go to Naples". A. said "Why not Naples then" & E. brightened from *terrible* depression and took passages for Naples next day'. On Friday 31st, therefore, they both left for Tilbury and boarded the *Osterley*. By Wednesday February 5 they 'began to like several people' and to play quoits on deck. The following day they landed at Toulon, where they walked about the fine harbour and looked at the splendid battleships. On the 7th they sailed through the straits between Corsica and Sardinia. Alice enjoyed the beautiful sights, but Elgar was busy playing games on the upper deck nearly all day. Next day they docked at Naples and went to Parker's Hotel, where they had stayed in 1907, but according to Alice there was 'only a dull room left for us'. On arrival in Naples, Alice's diary is left completely blank, so it is difficult to know how they spent their time, although during this holiday Elgar did begin to write some sketches for *Falstaff*. From February 16—23 they were in Rome and then returned home by train through France. Before they left, however, they received the news that Julia Worthington was dying of cancer.

United States of America

The first time the Elgars visited the States was in June 1905. The Apollo Club of Chicago had given the first performance of *Gerontius* in America in 1903 and the following year it was given at the Cincinnati Festival. It was these two successful events which paved the way for the visit. They sailed from Dover on June 9 on the *Deutschland*, but at first they found the vibration of the ship dreadful and Elgar was unwell, so that Alice had to lunch at the captain's table alone on the 10th. However, by dinner he was feeling better and for the rest of the trip they enjoyed the sea and the pleasant weather. When they arrived at New York on the 15th they were 'much impressed' with the harbour and the magnificent river. They stayed overnight in the Manhattan Hotel and the following day went on to New Haven. The weather was unbearably hot and Elgar was ill enough for two days to have a visit from the doctor. But the weather changed and they went further up the coast to New London by train for a few days.

On June 28, Elgar received an honorary degree from Yale University at New Haven. They had gone over as guests of S S Sanford, Professor of Music at the University, and struck up a great friendship with him. Alice recorded that it was a 'very interesting & dignified ceremony'. (On his return home Elgar wore his degree gown when he was given the Freedom of the City of Worcester on September 12.) The day after the ceremony Elgar was again 'very poorly', however, and the weather became suffocating again. They enjoyed a day driving out towards the Blue Mountains, but the heat became too unbearable for them. Back at the Manhattan Hotel in New York they had a state room on the twelfth storey with an electric fan, and as the bedroom was too hot, Alice slept on the sofa in the sitting room.

They left New York on July 11, having had to queue for a long time to get on the ferry from the pier. Eventually, having reached the ship, they were displeased with their cabin, so Professor Sanford arranged to have it changed. The journey home was lovely — calm and warm — and they enjoyed watching the flying fish and porpoises and even saw a shark. On the morning of the 17th they were up early to finish packing and eventually arrived home at 4.30 pm.

In order to return the compliment for his degree, Elgar dedicated his *Introduction and Allegro for String Orchestra* to Professor Sanford:

Here is my exercise for the degree you have so kindly bestowed. Not at all what you expect to receive from an examinee, I'm afraid. You will think it perhaps unduly free and audacious. I could have sent you a more 'correct' exercise, but it would have been so much the less alive. I should not have been worthy of your honour if, after having received the degree, I had given you a stone. I can at least say that this work is a living expression of thought & sensations, & in that I hope you will find a hint of gratitude for the kindness which has welcomed me in your country.

* * *

During his visit in 1905 Elgar had discussed an invitation to conduct at the Cincinnati Festival of 1906, and the Elgars returned therefore the following year in order to fulfil this engagement. They left on April 6. Carice and May Grafton saw them off at the station and Alice noted: 'May very tearful — C. a little pale but quite composed — though I know her heart was full'. From Liverpool they sailed on the *Celtic* and had a comfortable cabin. Most of the trip, however, was windy and often the seas was rough, waking them many times in the night. Contrary to his earlier voyages, Elgar found the whole thing dull, although on a sunny morning the day before they arrived he did play games on deck. They docked on the 15th and travelled to Cincinnati, but Alice was not impressed — 'all wooden houses and hideous towns'. On arrival at Cincinnati the house where they were to stay was strange, large and empty, although the 'shower bath with pale glass door' did seem to appeal! In the following days, however, they were often disturbed by their noisy neighbours.

The rehearsals for *Gerontius* went fairly well but after the splendid performance Elgar heard that his father had died. On May 2 he conducted the first American performance of *The Apostles*. This was a fine concert. According to Alice: 'E. conducted splendidly & the impression was profound — Great Audience'. The following day there was a performance of the overture *In the South*. In the *Cincinnati Post* of May 1906 Elgar was described as 'the typical Englishman, silent, reserved, unsocial — until after dinner'. Lady Elgar came off better: 'small, plump, with laughing blue eyes and the prettiest manners imaginable'.

On May 7 they set off to Buffalo in order to see the Niagara Falls, which they visited the following day. This they found 'most, most wonderful' and went down by lift to go underneath the water. They 'looked out at occasional openings & saw the marvellous rush of green waters & mist.' Returning to New York, they spent a week with

Postcard sent by Elgar to Carice from New York, 1906.

Julia Worthington, whom they had met the previous year, at her home 'The Wyoming', 853 Seventh Avenue. One excursion that Alice enjoyed with Pippa, as they called her, was to Tiffany's and they all paid a visit to the Lyceum Theatre. Alice wrote to Jaeger from here on May 11:

> You will like to hear the Festival was a most satisfying success & E.'s works made the most *profound* impression ... Do you know *1200* people stood on the Gerontius night in the hall — It was a wonderful sight.

They sailed home on May 18 but there was rain and thick fog on the return journey and again Elgar was dreadfully bored. On arrival at Liverpool they took the ferry to Birkenhead before thankfully arriving back at Plâs Gwyn on the 27th.

* * *

Elgar returned alone to the States on March 2 1907 on the *Carmania*, only five days after his return from Italy. Alice had to remain at home to look after Carice, who had developed rheumatic fever. This time he appeared happier with the journey and Alice 'had 3 letters, all so dear & happy from E. Delighted with Carmania & his state room'. However, although the trip began well, they were delayed by gales when trying to enter New York harbour.

In New York, Elgar conducted performances of *The Apostles* on March 19, when Alice at home was 'thinking & thinking of E.', and *The Kingdom* on the 26th, which was 'very fine'. Whilst he was there he was asked to lead a prayer meeting to pray for the failure of *Salome* by Richard Strauss. Needless to say, he refused. (He recounted this story to Delius on his visit in 1933). During this visit he also conducted in Chicago, Cincinnati and Pittsburgh. The honorary degree of LL.D. (University of Pennsylvania) was conferred on him on April 13 at Pittsburgh, the day after a performance of the *Enigma Variations* there.

He left for home on the *Campania* on April 20, arriving safely back in Hereford seven days later. On his return home he wrote to Jaeger on May 28:

> I had a mixed time in America — mostly pleasant but the unpleasant times were jokable, so all passed well.

The next month he wrote again:

... how I did make 'you' sound in Chicago! A fine orchestra (100) & they knew (via dear Old Theodore Thomas)[1] *everything* of mine backwards: I shed a tear over it.[2]

* * *

In 1911 Elgar returned, again alone, to the USA, to conduct the Sheffield Choir, who were on a Coronation tour of the New World. He had agreed to conduct *Gerontius* and *The Kingdom*, but as Professor Sanford was now dead, he was not looking forward to the visit. Nevertheless, he left on March 25 and telegrammed to Alice from Queenstown, on the coast of Cork, that all was well. He also sent Dorabella a card from here showing a picture of a Cunard liner and with one word written on it — 'Goodbye'.

At the beginning of April they were in Canada and Elgar cabled home from Toronto, where he was to conduct *Gerontius*, that it was icy cold and he was hating it. A few days later he was amongst friends in New York, but from Buffalo Alice received another letter stating that he was 'hating it all so much'. The next stop was Cincinnati, where Elgar conducted *The Kingdom* on the 22nd, and from here Elgar wrote to Alice Stuart-Wortley: 'I long to be back & forget this worse than nightmare'. Indianapolis, Chicago, Milwaukee and St Paul were also visited before the return trip to New York at the beginning of May.

During the visit he worked on the *Coronation March* and an *Offertorium* for King George V's Coronation and also accepted an invitation to be the permanent conductor of the London Symphony Orchestra for the 1911–12 season, as Richter had retired. On May 3 he set sail on the *Mauretania*, arriving safely back in London on the 9th. Alice had rented a house at 76, Gloucester Place, and Elgar returned here in order to attend the first performance of the *Second Symphony* later in the month and to take part in the various festivities for the Coronation.

---

[1] Conductor of the Chicago Symphony Orchestra
[2] On reverse of paper programmed C.A.E. with note from Lady Elgar, June 1907

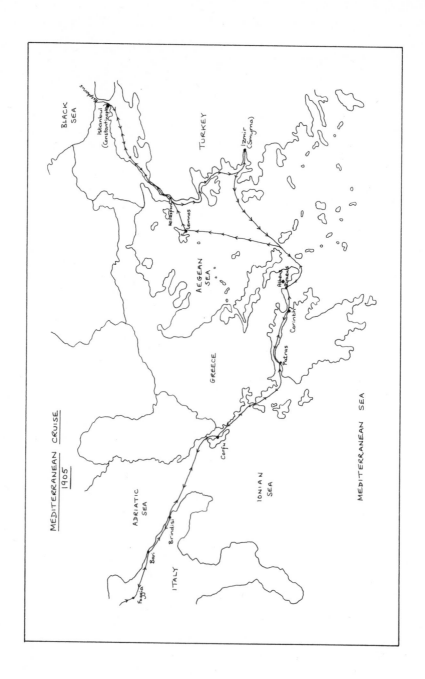

MEDITERRANEAN CRUISE
1905

BLACK SEA

Bosphorus

Istanbul (Constantinople)

TURKEY

Izmir (Smyrna)

Mt. Athos

Lemnos

AEGEAN SEA

Athens Piraeus

Corinth

GREECE

Patras

Ionian Sea

Corfu

IONIAN SEA

ADRIATIC SEA

Brindisi

Bari

Foggia

ITALY

MEDITERRANEAN SEA

Mediterranean cruise

In September 1905, Frank Schuster invited Elgar to accompany his party for a month's holiday cruise on HMS *Surprise* in the Mediterranean. Elgar accepted and throughout the cruise wrote a daily record in an exercise book which he bought at Corfu and which cost fourpence. The party were friends of Admiral Lord Charles Beresford, who was Commander-in-Chief of the Mediterranean Fleet, and included Sir George and Lady Maud Warrender and Lady Charles Beresford. Elgar was seen off by Alice, Julia Worthington, Mrs Gandy (an acquaintance from the Morecambe Festival), Canon Gorton, May Grafton and Carice.

He left Worcester by train on September 15 at 2.45 pm. The following morning at 9 am they sailed to Calais and then boarded the P. & O. Mail, in which they crossed France and travelled through Italy, arriving in Brindisi in Southern Italy at 8 pm on Sunday the 17th. They were expecting to sail on an Austrian Lloyd ship, but finding that there was no ship leaving, they had to go in a small Italian steamer. Arriving at Corfu at 9 am the following day, they all went ashore in small boats.

On Tuesday September 19 they arrived at Patras in Greece and took a train to Athens. At the station they were worried by crowds of beggars, but they had glorious views of the Gulf of Corinth on the journey. They continued to Piraeus and then walked to an electric station and went on to Phalerum Bay, Piraeus, where the fleet was. Here they boarded the *Surprise* and were met by Lord Beresford and Captain Bruen. The diary reads:

> Saw the Doctor had some tea & toast, & later some beef tea; & then slept 12 hours. Deo Gratias.

The following two days (20th and 21st) were spent ashore, visiting the Acropolis, the museum, shopping and paying a visit to the British Embassy for tea. On the 22nd the fleet sailed to Lemnos, where they arrived early the following morning. Here Elgar received a telegram which had come eight miles on a donkey. They went ashore and Elgar wrote:

> All Turks — poor dried up little village, quite eastern — dogs about. We walked thro the village and out to open country. Heard a pretty shepherd boy playing on a pipe quite beautiful. (Saturday, September 23rd)

The fleet was not allowed to go near Constantinople, due to the

Akaba crisis; therefore they were only able to sail past the Hellespont to Tchanak and there had to board an Austrian steamer to take them to the capital. During the night they ran down a large boat with no lights and several men were drowned. On Monday 25th they arrived at Constantinople, where they booked in at the Perah Palace Hotel and the following day visited the Church of S Sofia, went to the bazaar and then drove around the old walls. On Wednesday they were entertained in Turkish fashion at the Seraglio and re-visited the bazaar, where Elgar bought a pipe mouthpiece and an icon. He heard the call to prayer from a minaret near the bazaar which must have greatly impressed him. An attempt was made to blow up the Hotel Kroeker, patronised by the English and the French, when Elgar and Schuster were passing. That evening they sailed up the Bosphorus.

The next morning (Thursday 28th) they visited the Embassy for lunch and left Constantinople in the afternoon on the Mauritius steamer *Yangtse* for Smyrna, where they arrived at 2 pm on the Friday. The fleet arrived later and they boarded the *Surprise* once more. Elgar's diary reads:

> Rose early — glorious day. Frank, Lady M.[1] & I ashore went to the bazaar. Much finer sight than Constantinople. Colour, movement; & camels — 100's — led by a donkey through the bazaar. (This was my first touch with Asia & I was quite overcome.) The endless camels made the scene more real than in Stamboul. The extraordinary colour & movement, light & shade were intoxicating. Lady M. & Frank bought heavenly jam (cherry & *roseleaves*) & camel-bells, rugs & coverlets.) Lady M. gave me a silver camel lamp in remembrance of my first eastern camel.

In the afternoon they drove around the ancient town. The Sunday (October 1) was very hot, with a sirocco wind blowing. Elgar bought a *Red Letter New Testament* (he annotated this copy, which replaced one he had lost, for the libretto of *The Kingdom* and his third — unfinished — oratorio). After lunch the party visited the mosque of the dancing dervishes, but Elgar was more impressed with the music than the dancing. On the Monday they visited the bazaar again and in the afternoon took a steam launch around the fleet. They were rewarded with beautiful views of Smyrna, but Elgar had drunk some foul water and felt unwell. The following day they left Smyrna at 5 am but the weather broke and they all felt ill.

On Wednesday October 4 they passed through the canal into the Gulf of Corinth and arrived at Patras in rough seas. They landed and

---

[1] Lady Maud Warrender

IN SMYRNA

EDWARD ELGAR

went to the hotel with no prospect of a steamer until the Saturday. On the Thursday they visited the old castle which was part prison and part garrison. Elgar bought a roughly carved knife from a prisoner. The following day he bought a dagger, then drove through beautiful countryside where grapes, currants and olives were growing in abundance.

They left Patras on Saturday evening at 9.30 pm and arrived back at Brindisi in Italy at 5 am on Monday October 9. Here they had to wait twelve hours for a train. It finally left at 5.03 pm. At Bari they rushed out for some soup and by the time they reached Foggia, where there was some commotion by people wanting to board the train, it was much cooler again. On the following day Elgar and Schuster parted at Bologna, as Schuster was going to Venice and Elgar continued to Milan, where he saw the cathedral and La Scala. He travelled through France on October 11 and had a rough crossing from Calais, arriving at 4 o'clock the next morning in Dover. He then caught a train to London and stayed at the Langham Hotel overnight. On Friday October 13 he had to travel to Norwich for a rehearsal of *The Apostles* and finally on the Saturday travelled via London back home to Hereford.

After his return, Lord Beresford wrote to Elgar to tell him that his bandmaster was several inches taller — 'since your kind notice of him'. During the voyage Elgar had dined with Lord Beresford on his flagship *Bulwark* and the band had played *Salut D'Amour* and *Serenade Lyrique*. Lady Beresford requested that Elgar should write something for her as a remembrance of the trip. The result was the piano piece *In Smyrna* inspired by his visit to this colourful and exciting place and in particular his visit to the Turkish Mosque. As Dr Jerrold Northrop Moore has said:

> *In Smyrna* is an exquisite pastel — the purest piano expression he ever achieved.

The Low Countries

Elgar's first visit to Holland was in December 1904, when he travelled to Rotterdam for a performance of *The Apostles* on the 2nd and visited The Hague before returning to Germany.[1]

* * *

On August 10 1908, Elgar and Alice travelled to Ostend so that Elgar could conduct some performances of his works. They stayed at the Hotel du Place, and although they disliked the hotel they were given a great reception by the Belgians. At the rehearsal the day after their arrival the '... Orchestra gave E. a fine reception & applauded at the end of many things'. The following day they were said to be 'mad about the Variations'. On Friday August 14 a special Festival Concert was given to honour Elgar. The musical director of the Kursaal, Léon Kinskopf, was the main organiser of the event. Eminent Belgian composers and also Vincent D'Indy and Edgar Tinel were invited to meet Elgar. When he appeared to conduct the concert, which included *In the South*, the brass section of the orchestra greeted him with a brilliant ceremonial fanfare. At the end of the concert 7000 people stood to applaud him and to honour the National Anthem. Alice wrote that it made her 'proud to be English'. They sailed home the next day, having had a wonderful five-day visit.

* * *

In March 1911, Elgar went to Belgium to conduct a large Elgar concert to be held on the 12th, which had been arranged by the Belgian violinist Ysaÿe. He left for Brussels on March 8 and was pleased with the rehearsals. One of the afternoon rehearsals was open to the public at the Alhambra Theatre and was crowded. Elgar was delighted and there was great applause when during the *First Symphony*, which Elgar conducted, Ysaÿe sat down to play at the first desk as a member of the orchestra. Elgar also conducted the *Violin Concerto* with Ysaÿe as soloist. The concert was a great success and Elgar travelled back to London the following day very happy with his trip.

* * *

---

[1] See under Germany, p 101

On November 15 1919, Elgar left for Brussels and then went on to Amsterdam to conduct a concert with the Mengelberg Orchestra on the 20th. The concert included *Cockaigne*, the *First Symphony* and the *Violin Concerto*, and the orchestra gave Elgar a great ovation and asked him to return to conduct again the following year. The critic in *De Telegraaf* wrote a long article, stating that the style of Elgar's music was cosmopolitan.

He then returned to Brussels to conduct again and to be the guest of the Belgian Minister of Justice. This visit was arranged by Vandervelde (son-in-law of Edward Speyer), and who also arranged that he should be honoured for *Carillon*, his tribute to the Belgians. Elgar thus became the guest of honour at a reception held at the Ministry of Justice, was entertained by Burgomaster Max at the Hotel de Ville and was taken around the battlefields. He also drove to Antwerp one day for lunch with a banker called Strauss. On the one hand he thought the Belgians gay, apparently wealthy and with great enthusiasm for eating, but in a letter to Troyte Griffith after his return home on the 27th he wrote:

> The Belgians are putting up the most awfully shoddy ugly & degraded buildings (Louvain etc.) in place of the old, destroyed houses — the suburbs of, say, Wigan are noble compared to these atrocities. The B's swagger & do nothing but eat & drink — have forgotten the war & seem to detest the thought of English![1]

* * *

Elgar was honoured with the 'Ordre de la Couronne' from the Belgian King Albert on June 12 1920, shortly after Lady Elgar's death. As he was unwell at the time, Carice went to the Embassy to collect the insignia for him.

On October 1 he had to travel to Amsterdam and Brussels for further conducting engagements which had been contracted before the death of his wife. He returned on the 24th. One thing delighted him on this visit: a trip to Antwerp he visited the Musée Plantin and was able to touch a printing machine. These had always fascinated him since the days of his visits in his childhood to the printing works owned by the Leicester family, neighbours of the young Elgar in Worcester.

---

[1] Letter dated December 8 1919

South American cruise

In November 1923, whilst living at 'Napleton Grange' in Kempsey, Elgar, feeling in need of a complete change and longing to escape the English winter, decided to take a cruise to South America. He had thought of travelling to Italy or Egypt, but did not want to go alone. When a travel agent suggested the idea of a South American cruise the idea appealed, and as vacancies were available Elgar booked a passage. His friend Sybil Buckle (from whom he was to rent 'Battenhall Manor') had previously made the same journey and this could also have influenced his decision. A cruise aboard ship, with the company it offered, was ideal for him.

He sailed from Liverpool on the *Hildebrand*, a small ship of 7,000 tons owned by the Booth Steamship Company. Elgar, usually a good sea traveller, preferred a smaller boat. Out from Liverpool and into the Atlantic, however, the worst sea remembered for a decade was encountered, so that the Liverpool pilot who was usually put off at Holyhead had to be taken on to Madeira. From here they sailed to Para at the mouth of the Amazon. Elgar kept a tiny diary which has a few cryptic entries: Friday, 16th. 'Rough, not up'. Saturday 17th: 'Rough, not up'. Sunday: 'Dressed'. December 7: 'Crocodile'.

They sailed one thousand miles up the Amazon, as far as Manaos. Elgar enjoyed himself a great deal, becoming friendly with Mr Mandrell, the ship's commander. Although he kept himself away from foreigners, especially the Portuguese, he was pleased with the English company on board. He also entered with spirit into the many social functions arranged for the passengers. Despite the fact that there were 20,000 species of insect in the jungle, Elgar was very pleased with himself that he was never stung or bitten. According to W H Reed, the thing that seemed to impress him most was the fact that even in places with a relatively small population in South America, the opera house was always the most important building. After his return home he began to talk of possibly composing an opera. The cruise was completed at the end of December and Elgar, having thoroughly enjoyed the experience, was determined to go on the same trip again.

Coda

Elgar's favourite holiday haunts, to which he returned time and again, include his visits to Dr Charles Buck in North Yorkshire and his visits before and after his marriage to the Lake District. Other memorable holidays were those with Rodewald at Bettwys-y-Coed and his trip to Llangranog in 1901. The family holiday at Gairloch, in which they all delighted so much, was unfortunately spoiled by the outbreak of war. His special retreats for work and relaxation, where he returned for 30 years, were 'The Hut' at Bray and 'Ridgehurst' near Shenley. Abroad, the place dearest to the Elgars' hearts was Bavaria, where they returned for several successive years, and it was from these experiences that husband and wife were to share in their most intimate collaboration — the part-songs *From the Bavarian Highlands.* Italy was another beloved spot, especially Rome, which they adored.

Other families to whom the Elgars were grateful on many occasions, include the Fosters of 'Brockhampton Court' near Ross-on-Wye; Lord and Lady Charles Beresford of Brunswick Terrace, Brighton, where the Elgars spent the Christmas of 1911 and some days in 1919; and Mary and Antonio de Navarro, who owned 'Court Farm' at Broadway. Here, at this great social centre in the Cotswolds, the Elgars were entertained many times, 'Court Farm' was a Jacobean farmhouse at the foot of Broadway hill, complete with inglenook fireplaces and original oak beams. Mary de Navarro (who before her marriage had been the actress Mary Anderson) was a friend of Elgar's for 35 years. He gave her the baton with which he conducted the first performance of the *Violin Concerto.* Elgar spent many happy hours in the music room at 'Court Farm':

> We had an organ in the gallery of our music room, and there he went each evening as the sun began to set, asking me to blow for him while he improvised. Sometimes he liked what he was dreaming of, saying: 'I must do that again and try to remember it. Do you like it?'[1]

He also loved spending mornings by the swimming pool, which had been converted from a stagnant pond, and enjoyed his meals taken out of doors. He was determined to kick a football across the pool and expended much energy trying to do so. 'I bet a Sonata I'll get it across', he said, but he never did. Mary de Navarro wrote a touching tribute to Elgar in *The Times* (February 28 1934), entitled 'Lighter Moments at Broadway':

---

[1] *A Few More Memories*, Mary Anderson de Navarro, p 205

... he seldom passed our house on his journeys between Worcester and London without looking in, if only for a quarter of an hour. On his last birthday he appeared thus unexpectedly, looking radiant; he had just flown from France and was as excited about it as a schoolboy. He would frequently arrive with an unpublished record or two as a present. Once he came with the proof records of his magnificent *Falstaff* and marched about the room acting the part with much spirit, now and then breaking off to explain the different scenes portrayed in the music. Another time he brought us a record of Moszkowski's *Malagueña* and danced me wildly about the room while it was being played ... Two years ago John McCormack was staying with us and Sir Edward came over for a long day. He was in brilliant form. He played a great deal, with the orchestral effects that characterize a composer's piano-playing, and he accompanied McCormack in parts of Gerontius. It was an unforgettable day.[1]

After the death of Lady Elgar, Elgar himself naturally visited his daughter Carice, after her marriage to Samuel Blake, at her home 'Lockner', Chilworth, in Surrey. W H Reed, one of Elgar's greatest and most loyal friends, spent the latter part of his life at 'Froom', 33, Chatsworth Road, Croydon, and Elgar stayed with him here in May and June 1933.

Of his travels in Great Britain, none of the conducting tours Elgar engaged in around England have been included, except the Isle of Man and Morecambe, unless they have been mentioned fleetingly, as these require a volume in themselves. Elgar made several trips on tour to Wales. In April 1913, at the South Wales Music Festival, the Elgars attended concerts in Swansea, Neath, Mountain Ash and Newport. Lady Elgar was appalled at the concert hall in Maintain Ash, where Elgar conducted *King Olaf*, but found the chorus thrilling. In May 1920, Elgar went to South Wales for a tour with the London Symphony Orchestra, shortly after Lady Elgar's death, and in June 1924 returned for a tour of Central and North Wales and the fifth Aberystwyth Festival. On September 26 1906, Elgar went to Scotland to receive an honorary degree (LL.D.) at Aberdeen which Professor Terry had secured for him. In October 1909 he gave a speech at Aberdeen on the occasion of a complimentary dinner to Sanford Terry, which contained some radical ideas on the future of English music.[2] During the war, Elgar returned to Scotland on tour with the London Symphony Orchestra. They visited Edinburgh and Elgar and Reed took a taxi to Queensferry on the Firth of Forth and watched the cruisers being overhauled at Rosyth, across the estuary. Elgar only

[1] Quoted in full in *A Few More Memories*, op cit, pp213–5
[2] See *Musical Times*, January 1910

made one trip to Northern Ireland and this was in the autumn of 1932, when he went to Belfast to conduct the *Enigma Variations* and *The Dream of Gerontius*.

Looking back on Elgar's life, it is astonishing to discover how much he was on the move, not only travelling to changes of scenery, but also constantly changing his homes. Although travel by car and air was unknown in the first part of the twentieth century, it is fair to say that rail travel in this country and abroad was likely to be much more convenient in the Edwardian era than it is today, when even the smallest of towns boasted its own station. Nevertheless, the actual process of travelling must have been extremely time-consuming and often dirty and exhausting for the passengers. When flying to France, Elgar himself wrote to Adela Schuster, Frank's sister: 'It is wonderful to avoid changes, oily-smelling boats & the hundred other troubles of the channel crossing'.[1] The organization must also have been considerable, packing for lengthy holidays or conducting tours, especially when social etiquette demanded far more changes for clothing than is required today. In view of this it is quite amazing the number of complicated trips the Elgars undertook. It appears that Elgar's restless nature necessitated this constant upheaval and this in some way stimulated his creative process.

---

[1] *Portrait of Elgar*, op cit, p 323

Bibliography

Birney, Nan, *Bray Today & Yesterday*. Maidenhead and Trow bridge, 1973.

Bolitho, Hector, *Older People*. London, 1935.

Brayshaw, Thomas and Robinson, Ralph, M, *A History of the Ancient Parish of Giggleswick*. London, 1932.

Burley, Rosa and Carruthers, Frank C, *Edward Elgar, the record of a friendship*. London, 1972.

Elrington, C R (ed.), *Victoria History of the Counties of England. Gloucester*, Vol. 8. (A History of the County of Gloucester for the Institute of Historical Research.) London, 1968.

Fenby, Eric, *Delius as I knew him*. 2nd ed, London, 1981.

Hodgkins, Geoffrey, *Elgar's Visit to Llangranog*. The Elgar Society News Letter, May 1975.

Kennedy, Michael, *Portrait of Elgar*. 2nd ed, London, 1982.

Maine, Basil, *Elgar: His Life and Works*. 2 vols, London, 1933.

McVeagh, Diana M, *Edward Elgar: His Life and Music. London, 1955.*

Mitchell, W R, *Elgar's Friendship with a Yorkshire Doctor*. The Dalesman, Vol 40, No 9, December 1978.

Mundy, Simon, *Elgar: his life and times*. Tunbridge Wells, 1980.

Navarro, Mary Anderson de, *A Few More Memories. People and Things as I have seen them*. London, 1936.

Norris, Gerald, *A Musical Gazetteer of Great Britain & Ireland*. USA, 1981.

Powell, Mrs Richard C, *Edward Elgar: Memories of a Variation*. 2nd ed, London, 1947. *The Music Maker. Edward Elgar Centenary Sketches*. London, 1957.

Reed, W H, *Elgar*. London, 1939. *Elgar As I Knew Him*. 2nd ed, London, 1973.

Wood, Henry, *My Life of Music*. London, 1938.

Young, Dr Percy M, *Elgar O.M.* 2nd ed, London, 1973. *Letters to Nimrod from Edward Elgar* (ed.), London, 1956. *A Future For English Music* (ed.), London, 1968. *Letters of Edward Elgar and other writings* (ed.), London, 1965.

Index

148

WORKS